The New Psychology
For
Managing People

The New Psychology
For
Managing People

Mortimer R. Feinberg
Robert Tanofsky
John J. Tarrant

Prentice-Hall, Inc.   **Englewood Cliffs, N.J.**

Prentice-Hall International, Inc., *London*
Prentice-Hall of Australia, Pty. Ltd., *Sydney*
Prentice-Hall of Canada, Ltd., *Toronto*
Prentice-Hall of India Private Ltd., *New Delhi*
Prentice-Hall of Japan, Inc., *Tokyo*

© 1975 by

Prentice-Hall, Inc.

Englewood Cliffs, N.J.

Library of Congress Cataloging in Publication Data

Feinberg, Mortimer R
  The new psychology for managing people.

  Includes index.
  1. Psychology, Industrial. I. Tanofsky, Robert,
joint author. II. Tarrant, John J., joint author.
III. Title. [DNLM: 1. Psychology, Industrial.
HF5548 F299n]
HF5548.8.F373   158.7   74-32473
ISBN 0-13-615302-X

Printed in the United States of America

How the New Psychology
Will Help You Manage

The pace of modern business is fast. The stakes are high. The manager who aspires to greater success needs all the help he can get.

Within the past few years, there have been a great number of significant developments in the behavioral sciences that can help the manager to do his job better. But many of these findings are inaccessible to the manager. Now, within these pages, the manager can find all of the *new* approaches to handling people—set forth clearly and adapted to the requirements of today's executive and supervisor. A few examples can give some indication of the breadth and freshness of this book.

The manager can be authoritarian—tell people what to do and get them to like *doing* it. You can find out how in Chapter 1.

In Chapter 2, there is a new technique for breaking workers in right that calls for *imprinting* them with positive attitudes and correct procedures. One section of Chapter 3 explains how your team will perform better when you set up "impossible" goals for them to shoot at.

Chapter 4 will show how you can use the new concept of "energy curves" to get people to be more productive without paying them more money, while Chapter 5 sheds new scientific

7

light on the age-old mystery of what makes people tick. Here you will discover methods for understanding why people "blow hot and cold" and for predicting their actions, as well as additional techniques for effective motivation that do not require added payroll dollars.

Chapter 6 explores the findings of non-verbal communications specialists, and shows how you can use "body language" to get what you want and still keep people happy about it.

Decision-making is one of the most demanding tasks that the manager faces. Chapter 7 simplifies this challenge by telling you how you can play your hunches and still be scientific, and how you can find out all you need to know about a forthcoming decision with a minimum expenditure of time.

Chapter 8 presents some important and extraordinary new insights into ways of sizing up and resolving a crisis.

The need to handle face-to-face confrontation with finesse can be a make-or-break challenge for the manager. Just one of the sections of Chapter 9 gives a detailed, professional method for controlling an interview with sophisticated questions.

And Chapter 10 offers a guide through the mine field of dealings with the wide range of "problem people," with whom the manager must cope today. The authors of this book are in a unique position to analyze the mass of recent developments in management science, distill out what is really significant, and present it to the businessman in the form of concrete recommendations. Dr. Mortimer R. Feinberg is Professor and former Acting Chairman of the Psychology Department, Baruch College, City University of New York. Dr. Feinberg is president and co-founder of BFS Psychological Associates, Inc., a leading management consulting firm. He is well-known as a speaker, writer and television commentator on management developments.

Dr. Robert Tanofsky is Assistant Professor of Psychology, Baruch College, City University of New York, and vice president of BFS Psychological Associates. His articles have appeared in a broad spectrum of business and professional journals.

John J. Tarrant is a consultant and writer on the human-relations aspects of management. He has written seven previous books.

Mortimer R. Feinberg
Robert Tanofsky
John J. Tarrant

Contents

The New Psychology
For
Managing People

1

Using the New Psychology to Make Yourself a Manager Today's Workers Will Follow

A generation of executives has followed the injunction to "win friends and influence people."

This approach worked—and worked well. It is not working so well any more. Managers are finding that they *can* make friends among the people who work for them, but making friends is not the same thing as exerting influence. And the name of the management game is *influencing people to be more productive.*

So in recent years, management training has concentrated on various means of motivation. Executives have been presented with a multiplicity of things to say and do in order to motivate workers to greater effort. But the emphasis has remained on "winning friends." The manager is urged to always remember that he must be a "nice guy."

So we have the picture of conscientious executives who, when faced with the necessity to take action, sit and ask themselves: "Are my people going to like this? Will they accept it?"

This is complicated. It leads to vacillation and deferment of necessary action. Worse—there is now a mass of evidence to show that it *just does not work.*

So in this first chapter, we present reasons why the manager should establish himself not as "Mr. Nice Guy," but as a *firm leader whom people will follow*. And we present a plan that any manager, new or experienced, can follow to establish himself as this kind of leader. He does not need to possess the charisma of a Douglas MacArthur, nor does he need to become a louse. If a manager follows certain simple and specific guidelines he can achieve a *posture* of effective leadership; and when he has achieved that posture, he doesn't have to indulge in day-to-day worry about whether "they" will like what he does or not.

He will not only be a better manager. New findings indicate that his people *will like and respect him better*.

Here is *why*—and *how*.

HOW TO CHOOSE A LEADERSHIP STYLE

There was a time in the bad old days when the only form of motivation known to businessmen was to get bigger and better whips. Now, of course, the use of brute force is frowned upon. A man would probably lose his credentials in the American Management Association if he so much as laid a hand on a subordinate.

Well, what do we use nowadays instead of the bigger whips? A lot of people would say we use "psychology." When it's used this way, the word psychology carries more or less the connotation of "being nice." You must "establish rapport."

But "rapport" is still quite a broad term. Let's narrow it down. Recently there has been a good bit of discussion of leadership style for the manager. Should the manager be an autocratic leader or should he be a democratic leader? For most people— and for most executives, too—the answer is obvious. It is better to be democratic than autocratic. The values of democracy are part of our national and cultural heritage. We prize freedom; we scorn dictators and autocrats.

Translated into management terms, the democratic style of leadership has come to mean an emphasis upon understanding people as human beings; giving people a high degree of freedom in the working environment; and accomplishing objectives through persuasion and understanding, rather than through close supervision and the handing out of orders.

For an example of two different kinds of leadership in action, let's take a look at the contrasting approaches of two different managers. Their situations are somewhat similar. Each is working with a fairly young group of key people. Each group is college educated, intelligent and articulate. And each manager, with his particular group, faces the responsibility of accomplishing a difficult task in a relatively short time.

The first manager, Ray Watson, takes one approach. He begins by sitting down and structuring on paper the job that each of his key subordinates is expected to do. And he calls the group together, describes the objective to be obtained and outlines his general method of operation. He engages in a reasonable amount of discussion with the group, but he maintains fairly sharp limits. A given subordinate may choose among a number of options available to him in getting his part of the job done, but it is made plain to the subordinate that he is moving along a track which has been chartered for him by the manager. As the group moves into the execution phase, Watson "rides herd." He is constantly on the scene. He makes recommendations and he will listen to suggestions. Sometimes he accepts suggestions, but these tend to be of smaller rather than larger significance. In summation, Watson manages with a tight rein until the project is completed.

Dave Kennedy uses a different approach. His first move is to summon a meeting of all key subordinates. At the outset, Kennedy throws the meeting wide open by saying, "Here is what we have to accomplish. I'd like to hear all of your ideas on how we can go about it." Kennedy is very patient; he takes a lot of time to engage in a thorough give and take over each recommendation. Finally a plan is forged. Subordinates are given maximum latitude as to how they will accomplish their segments of the job. Kennedy is available, but as a resource and a troubleshooter rather than as a task master. As Dave Kennedy himself puts it, "These are well motivated people; I don't have to stand looking over their shoulders."

WHICH KIND OF LEADERSHIP WORKS BEST?

Now for some questions based upon the admittedly brief and sketchy narrative within each case.

> . . . Which of the two, Watson or Kennedy, is managing according to the generally accepted principles of modern management psychology?
> . . . Which of the two groups is more likely to get the job done—and done better?
> . . . Which of the two managers is apt to be better liked by his people?
> . . . Is Tom Watson a *task*-oriented or a *people*-oriented manager?
> . . . Is Dave Kennedy a *task*-oriented or a *people*-oriented manager?

Now for some answers. The first question asked which of the two managers, Tom Watson or Dave Kennedy, seemed to be following more closely proved principles of modern management. We asked a number of executives to read the brief cases and to answer the question. The great majority said that the second manager, Dave Kennedy, was following current approved practices in management. Why? Well, he is showing confidence in the *initiative* of his subordinates; he is asking and not *telling;* he is *working with* his people; he is *thoroughly* involving key members of his team in the task at hand.

The second question asked which group would get the job done better. Watson's group in which the tasks were highly structured and everyone was told what to do? Or Kennedy's group in which the objectives were stated and everyone was asked to participate in working toward a solution? The majority feel that the latter group—the more loosely reined group—would get the job done better.

Next question: Which of these two groups would like its manager better—the group which was closely structured, or the group which was given a great deal of freedom? That's easy—the consensus is that the loosely structured group has a higher degree of respect and affection for its manager.

As for the last two questions, the answers seem fairly obvious. Tom Watson, the "taut ship" manager, is *task*-oriented. Dave Kennedy, the exponent of democratic leadership, is *people*-oriented.

So here we have a heartening picture. We see the manager who is a "nice guy," and "treats his people like grown-ups," working in easy association with key subordinates as they move toward a common goal. They are all participating, "they are all working together." The manager does not dictate; he does not "pull rank."

Now let's take a look at how closely this picture approaches reality. For these two brief cases have not just been pulled out of the air. Though highly capsulized, they represent real situations. Furthermore, they represent two typical management approaches. Moreover, the attitudes reflected in the answers we got are also typical. There is a considerable tendency among managers today to approve of democracy in leadership and to disapprove of autocracy. Even when there is agreement that a highly autocratic manager is effective ("he's a louse but he sure gets the job done"), at the same time there seems to be an implication there is something not quite respectable about the taskmaster. Along with this we find the thought—perhaps it is a consoling thought—that "riding herd" may work over the short pull, but over the long haul it is bound to fail, because the manager fails to achieve rapport with his subordinates.

As a matter of fact, in the instances cited, the group which was tightly managed by Tom Watson got the job done faster and better. That may not come as any bombshell. But now add this: the subordinates reporting to Tom Watson, the "tough" manager, are shown to have a much higher regard for him both as a leader and a person than Dave Kennedy's have for *their* manager. This, in spite of the fact that Kennedy encourages participation, permits his people to structure their own jobs to a high degree, and allows them to solve problems on their own. We have seen this pattern recur over and over again.

NEW DISCOVERIES ABOUT LEADERSHIP

As a matter of fact, industrial psychologists and behavioral scientists are beginning to come up with some new and startling findings on this question of structured versus permissive leadership. Here is a typical experience related to us by Dr. Henry Tosi of Michigan State University. For a long time Dr. Tosi has shared with management thinkers and executives a set of assumptions which has shaped much of our modern approach to leadership. Dr. Tosi "bought" some of the opinions about tight rein versus loose rein management which a good many of us have shared up until recently.

On the basis of these assumptions, Dr. Tosi set out to conduct an important experiment in management. He wanted to see if productivity could be upgraded by matching subordinates with a *high* regard for freedom with managers who were willing to bestow maximum freedom. At the same time the study, which covered 500 managers, matched subordinates who had a high need for *structure* and *direction* with managers who were inclined to hold a tighter hand on the reins.

The feelings of managers and workers about freedom in the job were ascertained through standard tests that measure the individual's relative affinity for authoritarianism. Then the match-ups were made. At the same time there were control groups— "high freedom" employees with "low freedom" managers, and vice versa.

Here, capsulized, are the results. Subordinates with a high need for structure preferred the highly-structured boss. Predictable so far.

But, those subordinates who had manifested a high need for *freedom* also preferred the *highly-structured* boss to a significant degree.

So the congruence pattern that Dr. Tosi had hoped to establish did not work out. But in the course of his research he came upon findings that may have considerably more impact for managers.

Employees who value guidance above freedom prefer managers who run a taut ship. Employees who value freedom above guidance *also* prefer managers who run a taut ship.

Of course, Dr. Tosi probed for the reasons why. Some interesting points emerged. For one thing, employees did *not* view laissez-faire leadership as freedom. Rather they tended to perceive it as a *lack of interest* on the part of management.

Employees—even the most freedom-loving employees—felt that they enjoyed greater participation with the tougher boss than with the more democratic boss. They had something solid to bump up against; you can't bump up against a feather pillow.

So it seems that people who work for the "tougher" boss not only get the job done better, but they like the boss better. This is a growing phenomenon, and it will continue to grow. Authoritative research, conducted among the young people now moving into jobs, shows that these young people draw a distinct line between freedom *off* the job and freedom *on* the job. Off the job they want to be free to do their thing. They are not willing to "eat, sleep and live" the company. But *on* the job it's a different story. They desire and expect structure, guidance and direction. They want leaders who tell them, very clearly, what to do. When the boss asks such people: "Well, how do you want to do it?"— they are not inspired. Rather, they are frustrated.

Now let's move on to the last two questions which we posed— about whether these two managers were task-oriented or people-oriented. The evidence is pretty clear about the respective orientations of Tom Watson and Dave Kennedy in *these specific instances*. But to say that Watson and Kennedy are task-oriented or people-oriented in their overall approach to management would be going too far. We do tend to place managers in these categories, but recent evidence shows that this is a mistake.

We all have a tendency to "type" people. We meet a man who says little, and smiles not at all. We put him down as a quiet, mirthless individual. Actually, most of the time he may be a gregarious, humorous person. For some reason he was not that way when we were introduced to him.

The findings of behavioral scientists may sometimes seem to fall into this pattern. When we talk about "democratic leaders" and "autocratic leaders," for example, there might be an impression that people remain in such categories permanently.

Not so. And we have fresh evidence of this in some interesting new findings disclosed by Dr. Fred G. Fiedler.

Dr. Fiedler has been conducting extremely important research in management leadership for some years. We have referred before to his observations on the task-oriented manager and the people-oriented manager.

For simplification in reporting of research, these terms are frequently used abstractly. But it would be wrong to conclude that a given individual is *always* task-oriented or *always* people-oriented.

As a matter of fact, Dr. Fiedler has found that managers will change these roles—and change them in a predictable way. When confronted with a problem, a manager who is task-oriented is likely to change over to being people-oriented when the problem is solved. In effect he says, "We've got that straightened out, so now I can get to know my people better."

By the same token, the manager who is *people*-oriented at first will often become *task*-oriented when things are going well. He seems to say, "My people are behind me now; they've proved it. Let's keep the job rolling."

So it is not germane to ask of a man, "Is he task-oriented or people-oriented?" He can be either. The better question is, "Does he choose the leadership style that best fits the current situation?"

SOMETIMES PEOPLE WANT TO BE TOLD WHAT TO DO

It begins to appear that the democratic "free rein" approach to management not only does not achieve better results, but does not even lead to employees' liking the boss better. But one might ask, isn't such "democracy" one of the principal tenets advanced by the great architects of modern industrial psychology, by such towering management thinkers as Dr. Frederick Herzberg and Dr. Abraham Maslow? These eminent men are often cited as leading advocates of the democratic style. But, as a matter of fact, both Herzberg and Maslow warn against carrying free rein leadership to undue lengths. One quote from Dr. Herzberg: "To expect individuals at lower levels in an organization to exercise control . . . is unrealistic. Thus, when participation is suggested in these terms, it is usually a sham."

The late Abraham Maslow, it is true, opposed rigid authoritarianism. However, Maslow made a basic assumption. He assumed that if a man gets to be a manager, there is a reason for it. One good reason is that he possesses an overall superiority to the people who report to him.

Heavy stress on participative management leaves out the vital fact that the manager is likely to think and act faster, and more effectively, than others. And this leads to problems. Maslow declared, "There is a special realistic situation which sometimes occurs, and which makes all of us democratic people very uncomfortable: the great factual superiority of a particular person over his colleagues. This tends to confuse the question of what is required in a situation, and the kind of leadership which should prevail.

"Discussion and participative management style is obviously less possible, or at least is more costly, in a situation where five people with IQ's of 120 are teamed up with a leader of IQ 160."

Conventional management wisdom dictates that the boss should talk things out, listen to everybody's ideas, and let people participate in slowly working toward solutions to problems. But the gifted manager pays a price for this. As Dr. Maslow points out, "For one thing, the superior person is apt to get extremely restless in such a situation, and the strain upon his body is apt to be much greater because of the necessity for controlling himself and inhibiting his impulses. He may easily and quickly see the truth that all the others are struggling toward very slowly, and keeping his mouth shut can be physical torture."

Phony equalitarianism makes it tough for subordinates as well. They know the boss is likely to reach the finish line before they are halfway around the track. So what happens? "They are less apt to work hard because the work is useless and senseless. Why should they sweat for three days to work toward the solution of a particular problem when they know all the time that the superior one can see the solution in three minutes? The tendency, therefore, is for all the others to become passive. By contrast, they feel that they are less capable than they actually are, and more stupid, too."

So don't listen to those who say, "Don't take yourself too seriously. You're a peacock today but a feather-duster tomorrow." You are a manager. And unless you are burdened with an extraordinarily weak ego, you must admit to yourself that you are superior.

Your superiority is based on more than intelligence and experience. Dr. Maslow points to another kind of strength—"the greater-than-average ability to tolerate anxiety, depression, and anger."

HOW TO AVOID PHONY EQUALITARIANISM

Too many managers continually act the central role in a drama that is the direct opposite of the tale of the Emperor's New Clothes. They pretend that they have no clothes on at all, when actually they are clad in regal garments.

The point is clear. You are a manager. You achieved that responsibility because you have ability. Use your ability. Manage. Don't hold back under the mistaken notion that you have to gear yourself to the least common denominator of the group.

But, of course, the manager who recognizes his superiority—and acts on it—also recognizes that he must build people. You don't want to stifle your subordinates. Here Dr. Maslow has a suggestion. To avoid overpowering the people who work for you, *stay away from them.* Let them conduct group discussions in your absence. They will "talk much more freely, be themselves more freely, actualize themselves more freely" when you are not around. You are freed of the necessity to "play dumb," and you can use the time more creatively. Some executives think that their role requires that they ask everybody's opinion about everything, before a decision is made. Here it is important that you separate the *need for input* from the *pretense of democracy*. To make sound decisions, you need information and suggestions. Get them by talking with people. But, when you have the information you need, don't play games. Dr. Maslow: "The strong man should also watch out for the trap of condescension, of phony discussions, of phony asking for opinions, of phony group dynamics. If the strong man knows the answer all the time and is simply trying to figure out some sly way of tricking the group into thinking that they have discovered it all by themselves, then most often it will not work and will simply breed resentments."

The company is not a social club. Everybody is there to get a job done. The manager who is good at getting the job done should not have to act apologetic about it. And he makes a mistake if he chooses a leadership policy on the basis of how well his subordinates will like him. Dr. Maslow says, "The stress should be on facts, knowledge and skill, rather than on communication, democracy, human relations, good feeling, and the like. There ought to be more bowing to the authority of the facts."

It is true that the Declaration of Independence says that all men are created equal. But Thomas Jefferson was not just "one of the boys," nor did he feel that he had to act as if he were.

You are a manager. You are not "just one of the boys." Your job is not to establish rapport, but to provide guidance and direction, and there is growing evidence to show that, in providing that guidance and direction, you will win greater rapport than if you had deliberately set out to seek it as your number one priority.

It is time for us to forget the terms "autocratic" and "democratic" in discussions of leadership style. Your style should be a *management* style, suited to the accomplishment of the job at hand. Broad outlines of the management style are these:

> . . . Determine your objectives.
> . . . Get enough input from your subordinates to make good decisions.
> . . . In broad terms, structure the job for the subordinate.

. . . Talk and work with subordinates to help them to do the best possible job.

This is our approach to a sound *management style* of leadership. It is not necessarily tough, but it is tough minded. It will serve as the basis of a great many recommendations to be made in this book.

HOW TO MOTIVATE PEOPLE
WITHOUT SPENDING MORE MONEY

It is totally unrealistic to enter into a lengthy discussion of motivation and management style without talking about money. Nowadays we hear a great deal about job enrichment, opportunity, recognition, satisfaction, and all the rest of it. However, in practical terms, the manager on the firing line knows that he can give broad and almost full recognition to a subordinate, offer wide opportunity for satisfaction through achievement, and undertake every conceivable effort to enrich the subordinate's job. Nevertheless, if another firm offers that subordinate $5,000 more a year and his present employer can't match it, that employee is likely to be gone, job satisfaction or no.

But money is not the whole story. There is a growing body of evidence to show that too many managers have gone beyond thinking of compensation as a very important factor in keeping people on the job and producing effectively. They have come to act as if money were the only consideration. There is recent interesting research that indicates the contrary; we would like to cite just one example. This example is not pitched at the management level. It is at the worker/supervisor level. But this does not mean that the research is not valid for higher echelons of the organization. Much of the most valuable research in industrial psychology takes place below the middle and top management level. Practically speaking, these are frequently the areas in which it is most feasible to conduct such research. While we must be careful in extrapolating from the lower to the higher level, there is nevertheless a point here that is important to any manager, whatever his rank.

Here is the case. It is described by Dr. Harold F. Rothe of the Beloit Corporation, Beloit, Wisconsin. The study was undertaken to determine the extent to which financial incentive plans have a negative effect on *consistency of production* among skilled workers. However, the results of the research shed some helpful light on the role of the supervisor.

A group of welders in a midwest manufacturing company had been on a financial incentive plan for a number of years. Then the union made a new agreement with the company and the financial incentive was removed. In the long run, the new arrangement meant more money for the welders; but in the short run their take-home pay was reduced.

Dr. Rothe instituted a study to find out what would happen to the productivity of the welders under these new circumstances. What would be your guess?

To answer in brief, output dropped immediately after the incentives were abolished. However, by the end of 48 weeks, production was back to the point at which it had been before the move. A primary objective of the study was measurement of the effects on *consistency of output* of the new plan. Events disclosed that consistency was *significantly increased*.

This finding agrees with our own observations of many pay incentive plans. They encourage people to work more productively when the need for money is greater—and to "coast" somewhat when financial pressure is eased. Obviously this makes it a good deal more difficult for management to forecast production and to plan accordingly. If planning is important, management must give some thought to the planning problems that may result from an incentive system and its concomitant variation of output.

However, even more interesting to us in this case is the finding that productivity increased—with consistency—after the initial drop. What took the place of the financial incentive to motivate the welders to turn out more work?

The management of the company maintained the old system of work measurement, even though the incentive factor was removed. Performance was measured against time study standards. The program of job tickets, routing sheets, etc. was kept going, and weekly production reports were prepared. But now, instead of using these reports as a basis for determining incentive pay, the foremen used these reports in discussions with the welders. Previously there had not been regular review of performance. Now there was.

Here is Dr. Rothe's observation:

"There is no proof, but it is believed that the incentives to work had changed from a financial one to social ones. That is, the foremen were now talking to employees about their productivity, showing them graphs of their performance, and exhorting them to produce . . . When a financial incentive system is in effect, *there is a tendency for foremen to act as expediters,* getting tools and parts so the operators can keep at their highly rewarded tasks. The foremen demonstrate relatively less leadership in that kind of situation than they do in a non-incentive situation. It is believed that in the situation studied here that *improved leadership methods provided the incentive to work that had previously been supplied by the financial incentives.*"

When the incentive plan was part of the picture, the supervisors assumed that it took care of motivation, thus relieving them of the task. What's left for the supervisor? He becomes kind of a glorified tool-room clerk, fetching and carrying so that the workers, spurred on by their desire for money, never run short of equipment or material.

But when the incentive is removed, the supervisors realize that they must move into the vacuum. So they begin to discuss production with the workers, and urge them to higher productivity. In other words, they *start doing their jobs as supervisors.* And the interesting thing is that *it works.* In this case productivity climbed back up, with the added benefit of *consistency.*

How about you. Pose yourself this question: suppose all expected raises were postponed? (As indeed was the case during the government's wage-price freeze.) Or even suppose that everyone had to take a 5% cut in salary? What would you do?

Well, you certainly wouldn't go on as if nothing had happened. You would. . .

    . . . spend more time with your people;
    . . . discuss objectives and performance with them to a much greater extent than before;
    . . . do everything you could to help them be more effective.

Well—what are you waiting for? Things that you would be doing under those circumstances are the things that you should be doing as a manager.

THE VITAL IMPORTANCE OF THE WORD "NO"

Here is a basic management situation. John Anderson has asked for a raise. His manager, Arthur Bradley, does not think that Anderson deserves the raise. Anderson is in Bradley's office and is about to get the word. This is one way that Bradley can begin to give it to him.

"John, I am very impressed with the work you've been putting in and your efforts to do the best possible job. However, as you know, this has been a difficult year for us. Everything is tight and, so much as I would like to do otherwise, I'm afraid that we will have to delay. . ."

Your imagination can reconstruct the rest of the conversation. Here is another way in which Bradley could open.

"John, after a great deal of consideration, I am afraid that I am going to have say no to your request for a raise. Here are the reasons why. . ."

Here is another management situation that comes up quite frequently. Manager Paul Williams has an eager subordinate named Ray Schultz. Schultz has put a great deal of time into developing a plan on which he is anxious to get his boss' okay. But Williams has considered the plan and decided that it will not work. Now Schultz is in the manager's office to hear the decision.

One way that Williams could handle it is this:

"Ray, I think your proposal has a great deal of merit. I am anxious to incorporate it as much as possible into our plan. Naturally, there will have to be some modifications, but as we move ahead. . ."

Here is an alternate method:

"Ray, you have put a great deal of thought and energy into developing this plan and I appreciate it. However, I'm going to have to say no to it. I'd like to tell you my thinking. . ."

In each of the latter alternatives, the manager levelled. He said what he really thought. He used the awful word, *no*. Having the guts to say "no," when that is what you mean, is important to the establishment of a position of coherent leadership.

The reason for this lies in a psychological phenomenon called *cognitive dissonance*. This term was originated by the psychologist Leon Festinger. It's worth knowing about because it applies to things we do as managers everyday. Festinger's theory is that the mind, when confronted with two sets of facts which create an uncomfortable psychological imbalance, adjusts these facts to make them more harmonious, and thus reduces the "dissonance."

Look at the two brief situations. In the first, the subordinate wants a raise. He has obviously convinced himself that he deserves the raise, and he expects to get it. If the manager hedges and stalls he has obviously not said yes to the raise. However, he has not said no either. Dissonance is created in the subordinate's mind. In the absence of a firm *no,* that dissonance will be resolved in favor of a *yes*. The mind is likely to operate so that in a week's time the employee understands and believes that the boss told him the raise would be forthcoming in a little while.

Cognitive dissonance will work the same way in the second situation. If the manager's rejection of the plan is unclear and cloudy, the subordinate's mind will resolve the dissonance in favor of a yes. In days he will be believing that his plan was accepted. We can easily envision the consequent confusion.

Why do so many managers dislike saying "no"? Well, we are all human. We don't like to disappoint people. But there is another factor. Some managers have been led to believe that they must go to great lengths "to keep employees happy" and part of the price of keeping people happy is never to say no.

Our research and observation indicate that this is a fallacy. People don't like to hear the word *no*. But they will accept it, and, overall, they prefer clarity to sugar coating. Clarity is one of the cornerstones to the position of viable leadership, and clarity often calls for a loud, clear no.

HOW TO GET THE
RIGHT KIND OF UPWARD COMMUNICATIONS

To achieve a sound position of leadership, the manager must assure himself of real communications with subordinates—not just routine reports; not just self-serving memos; not just things the employee guesses the boss wants to hear. But a lot of managers complain that this just does not happen. Why not? Let's look into it.

Here's what one executive said to us. "How can I get people to tell me what they are thinking? How can employees develop the ability to *pitch* the boss in a persuasive way so that he accedes to their ideas? Why aren't more people willing to *camp on the boss's doorstep* until they get through to him?"

This man is a progressive, intelligent, highly-capable executive. The problem he raises is shared by many company presidents and top managers. Management *needs to know* a great many things, and that need will not be satisfied if subordinates will not tell the boss what he needs to know.

We were struck by the way in which this executive formulated the questions, and the actual words he used. His words were typical of the way in which many managers view the problem. And we feel that in those very words lies a clue to the answers.

"How can employees develop the ability to *pitch* the boss. . .?" Obviously he was thinking of himself as someone who must be "pitched" to, or as a prospective customer for ideas who sits back and listens to a presentation.

Here is one manifestation of an attitude which acts as a deterrent to upward communication. A subordinate may be extremely valuable to the organization; he may have many thoughts about how the organization can function better. But his ability and ideas do not equip him to make a "pitch." He does not have the training, or the particular communication skills, to mount a compelling presentation in the way that the company's director of marketing or the advertising agency's account supervisor might be able to do.

But if this man's boss expects to be "pitched," that expectation has undoubtedly manifested itself to his subordinates. The implication is that the boss will be receptive, not only to ideas, but the method by which they are presented. The employee who is unable, or unwilling to take the time, to put together a full-fledged presentation will just keep his mouth shut. He is not going to risk humiliation and rejection by presenting his ideas in an inadequate way, regardless of how good as those ideas may be.

The manager asked another question: "Why aren't more people willing to *camp on the boss's doorstep*. . . ?" Our experience convinces us that, while many managers may in theory commend the employee who "camps on their doorsteps," in practice they consider such employees a pain in the neck. And indeed they are often right. A study conducted by BFS Psychological Associates showed that subordinates who were most likely to beard the boss in his den with suggestions were *not* the most productive and creative workers, but rather the most unhappy ones. They were coming to the boss, not to impart knowledge, but to take away reassurance.

Why should the onus of camping on a doorstep be placed upon the subordinate? If he is conscientious, he feels that he has a job to do, and that his time on the boss's threshold is time away from that job. Let's consider the problem as one of interaction between two people, regardless of status. The subordinate is working at his job, and quite possibly generating some ideas that may be valuable to his superior. The superior is trying to run an organization, and wishing that he could get more feedback from people down the line. When the situation is viewed this way, why should it be the subordinate's responsibility to camp on his boss's doorstep? The boss needs information and ideas; why should he not seek them out?

"Communication up" should not be "up" at such a steep grade; too many of those down below will conclude that it is futile and even dangerous to attempt the climb.

We find that people in an organization shy away from communication with superiors for three fundamental reasons:

. . . *They fear authority;* right or wrong, they conclude that unsolicited communication makes them vulnerable by placing them in an unpredictable situation with the man who can make or break them.

. . . *They are not convinced that they are right;* they feel that the boss has more facts at his disposal than they do (erroneous as this conclusion may be); and so, lacking an "ironclad" case, they stay away.

. . . *They reason that the risks of upward communication exceed the possible rewards;* the subordinate who pushes an idea that turns out to be *right* may receive recognition (which also reflects favorably on the boss's wisdom in employing him); but the downside risk of an idea that is *wrong* poses consequences that may be catastrophic.

The manager must face the fact that, however fair and affable he may be personally, his position creates barriers against upward communication. If he does no more than expect and exhort his subordinates to make superhuman efforts to scale those barriers, he is unlikely to receive very much creative nourishment from those who report to him. He should, rather, make it a part of his own responsibility to be accessible as a matter of course, and to *seek out* and *encourage* his employees to tell him what is on their minds.

SUMMARY—A FIVE-STEP PLAN FOR MAKING YOURSELF A LEADER TODAY'S WORKERS WILL FOLLOW

1. You decide what is to be done and make your decision clear to the group.

2. You structure the jobs of subordinates so that they can see the track they have to run on.

3. You let people know how they are doing, frankly and fully, at all times.

4. You say *no* clearly and forcefully when a no is called for.

5. You seek your people out to discover what they are thinking.

2

Apply the New Psychology to Establish Your Program

Some managers walk a tightrope. They worry about every action they take and every word they say. They operate in fear that one false move will throw into disarray their entire program. They "run scared."

But other executives move ahead confidently. They make mistakes, sure, without apology. They talk easily to colleagues and subordinates without being concerned about choosing words carefully. They change direction; adapt; modify instructions. They don't "run scared." And these are the men who get the job done easier and better.

What's the difference? The difference can be summed up in one word—*establishment*. The confident, effective manager is the man who has established himself and his program.

Let's take the typical situation of a new subordinate reporting to a manager. Let's examine ways in which different managers can handle this situation, and propose a plan by which the effective manager can best and most quickly establish his *policy*, his *authority*, and his *style*.

First we'll spend a few moments considering the state of mind of the new man—call him Bob Smith. Bob Smith is moving into a new situation. He is alert, keyed up, and on edge. He is forming impressions very rapidly. His mind is in a prime state for *imprinting*.

IMPRINTING YOUR METHODS ON OTHERS

"Imprinting," in the strict sense, refers to a phenomenon that behavioral scientists are learning more about. Experiments with this phenomenon have been conducted principally with lower animals and, particularly, birds.

Researchers have found that baby chicks newly hatched out of the egg are highly susceptible to imprinting. We have seen how small birds will follow their mother. It turns out that this happens, not because of some innate mystical quality of motherhood, but because the mother bird is the first object of any size that the fledgling sees. Experiments have shown that if a fledgling sees any sizeable moving object, such as a bird of another species, a human being, or even a football, he will follow that object indefinitely. This is called the process of "imprinting."

Something quite similar to the imprinting process takes place among human beings. When a person is under unusual stress, or when he confronts a new situation of some magnitude, the doors of his mind and emotions seem to open wide. He is "imprintable." The impressions that he picks up during this particular period will be deep and lasting. So here is the new subordinate, Bob Smith, confronting his new manager Ed Barnes. It's a new challenge for Smith; he is anxious, but he doesn't want to "put his foot in it." The impressions that he acquires *right now* will have a lot to do with how he does his job in the future. Ed Barnes, the manager, has a great deal of control over the imprinting process that is about to take place. Barnes can take advantage of this critical moment, or he can waste it.

What are the options open to Barnes as he interracts with Smith on the subordinate's first day in the new job? Well, Barnes might do what a lot of managers do. He may leave Smith pretty much on his own—"give the new guy a chance to settle down." Or, Barnes might be so concerned about Smith's anxiety that he will go out of his way to help the subordinate to relax. Some executives feel that a friendly chat about trivia is what is called for in this situation.

Other managers pick this time to do some selling. They want new subordinates to like the job, the department and the boss, so they talk to the subordinate about how superbly he is going to handle his assignments, how well he is going to get along with his colleagues and his superiors, and what a great place it is to work. In other cases, executives have a kind of a general, routine orientation that they give to everybody.

Now Ed Barnes *might* follow any one of these courses, or a combination of them. But, if he does, he will be wasting a matchless opportunity to establish himself with a man who is going to be working for him.

Or, let's face it, none of the approaches outlined above are going to do much to reduce Smith's anxiety. The new man is still going to be watching his steps carefully, afraid of making a mistake. As a matter of fact, we have often found that the more genially the boss "comes on" in this situation, the more anxious the new subordinate becomes.

But there is a more important point to be made. Even if there is a way to make the new employee relaxed, happy and friendly, *this is not the primary objective that the executive manager should be pursuing*. The manager should use this opportunity to *establish himself*—his policy, his authority, his style.

Now some executives feel that they do this by putting a new man right to work, and throwing him in on a "sink or swim" basis. There is no doubt that this will subject a subordinate to considerable stress, but it does not do much to establish the manager. Industrial psychologists have been giving a lot of attention to the critical period of first day orientation (obviously, new employee orientation can stretch on for days or even weeks; but it must be remembered that the period of heightened impressions of "imprintability" is very limited). And they have found that *neither* of the extremes—"take it easy and relax," or "get in there and start doing the job"—is particularly effective.

HOW TO BREAK PEOPLE IN RIGHT
—A SEVEN-STEP PLAN

The best way to break in a new employee is through an "integrated" approach. Begin to train the new man immediately and train him on the job; train him in a way that establishes *you* as you want to be established. Here is a seven-step plan that you can use to take advantage of "imprinting" in a way that will establish you with a new employee and get him producing fast—and the way that you want him to produce.

1. Lay out for him the general objectives and method of operation of the department as a whole. Be candid about your own desires and your own evaluations of how well or how poorly various parts of the overall job are being done.

2. Talk about his job and how it fits in with accomplishment of overall objectives.

3. Ask him a question. Pose a specific problem that he will be meeting in his job and to which he should be able to respond right now.

4. Discuss his answer. The discussion takes place within two contexts: one context is his own experience, capability and desire to do certain things his way; the other context is your general approach to how things should be done under your authority. The discussion should serve to bring these two contexts into one harmonious whole.

5. Cover other salient points of his job in the same manner.

6. Put him to work. This does not mean just turning him loose. Rather it means that you temporarily set up specific and formal points of feedback, discussion and review.

7. Use the feedback points to continue to organize your general approach with his specific ways of doing the job.

The manager who follows a plan like this will be going a long way toward establishing his policy, his authority and his style. He will be orienting the new subordinate in a way that is best designed to accomplish the manager's program and, as a by-product, he will be giving the subordinate greater security and an immediate feeling of understanding and respect for the boss.

The orientation of a new subordinate is just one situation in which it is important for the manager to establish himself. There are other such "new situations," such as when the manager's department must undertake a large new project, when the manager moves to a new department or a new job, or, indeed, when any new situation comes up requiring the manager establish himself as a leader. *Establish yourself first;* let everyone who is involved understand your feelings and your approach. *Imprint* your leadership on your subordinates. Then open the situation up to individual differences. When you have given the general guidelines and mapped the track on which people will run, you can stop worrying about what you say or do at any given moment of any given day. Your leadership is imprinted; your people will move ahead to execute your program the way you want it done.

FIVE GUIDELINES FOR ESTABLISHING YOURSELF

As you establish yourself and your program, you will at the same time be evaluating how well your efforts at establishment are going over. To some extent, this is a matter of "feel." The experienced and alert manager senses the degree to which he is in command. Nevertheless, here are five guidelines that will help you to use that sense most acutely in judging the extent to which you have established yourself with an individual.

1. *Does he understand it?* One of the best ways to test for understanding is by inviting questions. The individual who is "getting you" will have questions to shoot back at you. How sharp are his questions? Do they really help to clarify the situation? Does he flounder and dutifully come up with questions because he feels it is expected of him, or is he eager to ask questions so he can find out more? The quality of the questions you get back is one measure of your degree of establishment.

Carl Burke is instructing subordinate Rita Case on a project. Burke goes through the basics and then says, "I'm sure you have some questions, Rita." She thinks a moment, then says, "Yes, one or two. First, will you be notifying other departments about our plans?" Rita asks a couple of other questions, which

Burke answers. As he responds, he reflects with satisfaction that she has a grasp of the situation.

2. *Does he add "something extra"?* The steps you take to establish yourself and your program should not dull initiative. Rather they should sharpen it. Check to see if the individual adds to and elaborates on what you are telling him. He should be active, not passive. He should be building and not just absorbing.

Carl Burke, after answering Rita Case's questions, asks, "Do you have anything you'd like to add to this?"

She says, "Well, it seems to me that we might get extra mileage by. . ." And she goes on to offer some suggestions.

3. *Is he flexible?* The subordinate need not agree with everything you say to him in a new situation. You'll encourage him to respond and discuss particular points, and at the same time you will want to see how well he adapts to understanding your point of view. If he is "locked in" to a particular pattern, you should switch back to more general discussion that establishes the guideline within which you and he will operate.

Rita Case says to Carl Burke, "May I bring up one point of disagreement? I think it would be better if we conduct a running inventory. . ." She spells out her alternative. They discuss it and come to a conclusion.

4. *Is he enthusiastic?* Having gotten what he needs to know, is he anxious to get on with the job? You want the job done properly, but you do not want to discourage in any way the kind of enthusiasm and elan that impels a man to work on his own.

"Anything else?" asks Burke. Rita Case says that she thinks they've covered everything. Burke asks her when she plans to get started. With a smile she replies, "Right now!"

5. *Does he interact effectively?* The establishment of a relationship is a two-way street. You can't do all the work, the other party should be coming forward to meet you—and to establish relationships with others in the departments. Check the speed with which a new subordinate develops working interactions with you and with other people.

Evaluate as you establish. Check those five areas: quickness of understanding, flexibility, initiative, enthusiasm, and interaction. As you work to establish your program, you may want to jot down rough notes on key people under each of those five headings.

A NEW WAY TO PREDICT
HOW LONG PEOPLE WILL STAY WITH YOU

Effective establishment can become quite a chore for any manager if he is compelled to keep doing it over and over again. Consistently high turnover within a department can sap the impetus out of even the best conceived and established program.

Obviously, there is no sure-fire way to predict how long sub-ordinates will stay with you. There is no crystal ball into which you can gaze and say to yourself "three years," or "five years." However, the situation is not hopeless. Here is a description of a previously ignored clue that may help your predict the tenure of the people who work for you.

Most employment application blanks carry a space for "source of referral;" or "By whom were you referred"?—or something of that nature. This may be filled out, or it may not be. At any rate, nobody pays any attention to it. It is promptly forgotten.

Dr. Martin J. Gannon of the University of Maryland decided to find out whether source of referral had any relationship with job stability. He studied the records of a large bank over a four-year span. During this period the bank hired 6,390 employees; 1,934 terminated before completing their first year of service. Obviously a high and expensive turnover rate.

Dr. Gannon studied seven sources of referral, and he found that there was a *highly-significant difference in tenure of employees when they were classified according* to the referral *source.* Turnover percentages among the seven sources ranged from a low of 21% for the "best" source to a high of 40% for the "worst" source.

Before we go any further, why not try a little self test? We will list the seven sources of referral considered by Dr. Gannon. How do you rate them? Which source would provide the lowest turnover rate (highest stability)? Which would rate the poorest? How would the other rank in order of desirability?

Here are the seven sources:

Major employment agency (under contract with the employer)
Other employment agencies
High school referrals
Re-employed former workers
Referrals by present employees
Newspaper advertising
Walk-ins

Within these seven categories, here is the breakdown discovered by Dr. Gannon, beginning with the "best" (lowest quit rate) at the top:

Source of referral	# Hired	# Quit	% Quit
Re-employed former workers	253	54	21.3
High school referrals	602	131	21.8
Referrals by present employees	2320	615	26.5
Walk-ins	1212	349	28.8
Other employment agencies	637	241	37.8
Newspaper advertising	512	202	39.4
Major employment agency	854	342	40.0

This table is part of Dr. Gannon's report in the *Journal of Applied Psychology*, Vol. 55, No. 3.

The first and most obvious conclusion that might be drawn from these findings is that the employment agencies were not doing much of a job for the bank. But this would be superficial; other employment agencies would probably not do any better.

We feel that there are a number of profound points made by Dr. Gannon's results.

First, let us separate (as Dr. Gannon does) the four top-ranking sources from the three lower-ranking sources. There is a great difference. These four top sources—re-employed former workers, high school referrals, referrals by present employees, and walk-ins

—"can be considered as sources of stable employees." Conversely, the three low-ranking categories—other employment agencies, newspaper advertising, major employment agency—"can be viewed as suppliers of *unstable* employees."

Let's discuss a few observations on the reasons that underlie these facts. Re-employed workers were rated number one for job stability. And yet many companies cut themselves off entirely from this source. There is a policy, implicit or explicit, that no former employee should be taken on to the payroll again. But why not? Such a policy flies in the face of all present-day psychological concepts. It assumes that people can never change.

The employee who desires to come back to work for you after leaving you is likely to stay a good while, simply because he *knows the company*. There will be no tremendous surprises or disillusionments. He has seen other jobs or job possibilities—and he has decided that he is best off with your firm. He is a good bet to stay—and perform.

People who are referred by present employees are apt to have high job stability for several reasons. For one thing, the new employee does not want to embarrass the man who referred him by not performing or by quitting too quickly. The present employee who makes the referral knows the needs of the company (often better than management does), and he will not usually take the chance of lousing himself up by referring a poor candidate. And the older employee will often act as kind of an unofficial "big brother," counseling his protégé, calming him down, tiding him over discouragements, and giving him tips. (One caution here—this is fine if it takes place off the job. If the veteran employee takes time away from his own work to coach the newcomer, there can be a net loss in productivity).

High-school referrals rank high on this list of sources as pretty good bets for stability. Why? Well, it may be that someone at the high school was thinking about this candidate as an individual, and did some amount of preliminary screening in referring the person. Certainly, we can consider a high school referral as reasonable objective; the school's stake is in providing satisfactory workers, not just getting people hired.

Perhaps the most surprising thing about Dr. Gannon's findings is that "walk-ins" ranked significantly better than employment agencies or newspaper ads as a source of stable employees. Let's consider this. Employment agencies deal in bodies. They are paid on the basis of hiring, not tenure. By the very nature of their economics, employment agencies are not likely to be set up to select the workers who are most likely to stay on the job at your company.

And when openings are advertised in the newspaper, the employer is more or less dealing in bodies. He often does not do the screening job that might be done; and he is attracting people who happen to need work and who are reading the classifieds.

Contrast this with the walk-in. He is not sent by anybody, nor is he responding to a newspaper advertisement that says, in effect, "we need bodies." He has made a choice; he has chosen your company as a place he would like to work. Of course, it would be unrealistic to overstress this point; the candidate is applying at other places as well. But he *has* made a rough choice, so there must be something about your company that attracts him. In our judgment, Dr. Gannon's findings offer an important, simple and precise tool to managers who are concerned about job turnover. Has there been any effort made in your organization to tabulate early quits against sources of referral? Probably not. The information is not difficult to obtain, and the results of such a study could be extremely meaningful.

Does the company have a tacit policy against rehiring former workers? If so, maybe now is the time to ask what good this is doing, and weigh it against the possibility that such employees might be your most stable people.

Finally, we come to the question of employment agencies. We are not suggesting that business dispense with the employment agency as a source. But it might be a good idea to spend some time with your current agencies to find out how (or *if*) they screen people for you, to provide them with some fresh guidelines, and to let them know that their referrals are being measured in terms of job stability.

Also, there might be more emphasis on the obtaining of new

people through the recommendations of current employees. Here the question of a cash bonus comes up. We would be careful about paying employees to refer others; perhaps bonuses might be deferred until there is some judgement on the new worker's stability.

We recommend *source of referral* as a fruitful field of study for line managers and personnel executives who want to predict tenure and reduce turnover.

A NEW WAY TO EVALUATE YOUR TRAINING PROGRAM

Training is an integral part of establishment. You may not build the training programs for your organization, but you do depend upon the fruits of those programs and you should have something to say about the way the program is run.

Too much business training goes on, year after year, turning out a so-so product at a very high cost. Too many training programs continue to get a "free ride" because management has bought the idea that the effectiveness of training simply cannot be measured in any precise or reliable way.

Too often, training seems to be carried on, not as a means to a specific end, but just for its own sake. The training program is "just there," like the weather or the tides. There is nothing you can do about it, except to hope that the next product of the program who comes into your department is better than the last one.

It doesn't have to be this way. A training program *can* be set up to produce specific results. And it can be designed so that management *does* get measurable feedback that tells whether the program is paying off or not.

The *systems approach* is no longer a new development. It has found many highly-valuable applications in industry. But it has not been until just recently that there has been any consistent effort to design training programs according to a systems model.

As a matter of fact, engineers, the fathers of the systems approach, have been slow to modify their own basic education according to its principles. Not long ago, Dr. Louis T. Rader, Chairman of Electrical Engineering at the University of Virginia, urged at the annual meeting of the American Power Conference that the university preparation of engineers must be reviewed and overhauled from a systems point of view. Now engineers are beginning to apply their own discipline to their training, but for a long while the shoemaker's children went barefoot.

So it is not too surprising that more has not been done about shaping industrial training in useful system terms. Dr. Robert K. Branson, an educational consultant with headquarters in Walnut Creek, California, has provided us with some incisive thoughts about the systems approach to learning. We believe that his points can be applied with great effectiveness to the evaluation, design, and modification of business training.

First, let's define the systems approach in this context. Applied to training, it is a management tool calling for planning, design, development, implementation, evaluation and revision. (The last two functions, evaluation and revision, make the systems approach unique.)

A functional system has inputs, processes, outputs and feedback, all designed and integrated to accomplish a *specific mission objective*.

In an instructional system, the learner becomes an integral part of the system (not just a consumer of training). The system must update itself, and it does this on the basis of responses from the learner.

Each functioning component of the system must be designed in terms of the specific, measurable objective it hopes to achieve. *The system must deal only with identifiable objectives and goals*.

The last sentence is vital. Let's stop and consider a typical management training program. Ask the training director to describe it. Does he respond in terms of "measurable objective and goals"? Does he tell you what the program is designed to achieve? More often than not, he is apt to answer in terms of media—films, conferences, courses, sensitivity sessions, etc. (There was an unhappy time when "programmed instruction" was considered to be the epitome of the systems approach to learning.) Or, he may describe the structure of the program—"They spend three months in sales, three months in production, etc."

An astounding number of managers—line and staff—are not able to describe even generally, let alone precisely, *how the trainee is expected to behave at the end of the program that is different from the way he behaved at the beginning.* They know about the inputs, which are incidental; they don't know about the expected result.

According to the systems approach, a training program can be designed like a heating plant or any other system.

First comes a definite statement of the *mission,* or a statement of what the program is supposed to accomplish. This is critical; the description cannot be vague. It must be detailed and precise.

After the mission is defined, elements of the program are specifically described. *Each must be justified in terms of the mission.* Pseudo-justifications such as: "We have an excellent indoctrination film that cost us $50,000;" "It's most convenient to have them meet in the conference room every Friday afternoon;" "Some of our line managers are skilled in question-and-answer sessions"—cannot be accepted. Instead, descriptions should read like this: "After one day on the line, workers will be able to get their questions answered in a one-hour session with the trainer."

The system must be evaluated in terms of how well it is meeting the specified objectives—not in terms of how well people like it, or how closely it conforms to what is done in other organizations, or the degree to which it uses existing resources. What must the trainee be able to do? What should he know? The answers to these questions are built into the system at basic stages.

Choice of instructional media must always be made against one overriding criterion: accomplishment of the mission. And there must be follow-through at the end. The measure of the system is the effectiveness of its output. If a man who has come through the training program cannot do the job, he must be re-evaluated; *but the system must be re-evaluated as well.* How, after all, did the man get through?

Here are the steps in applying the systems approach to training:

a) Decide what behavior the trainee is to learn;
b) Plan instruction specifically to achieve performance objectives;
c) Measure carefully to find out how much was achieved;
d) Analyze the results to determine the causes of failure when it is found;
e) Revise the program to try a different approach when required;
f) Evaluate total progress against system objectives.

THE FOUR KEYS TO
ESTABLISHING YOUR LEADERSHIP

Establish your leadership by imprinting *your policy, your authority,* and *your style* on subordinates.

Evaluate the degree to which you are establishing yourself with each individual.

Estimate the tenure of the key individuals who will be carrying out your program.

Appraise your training plan according to the new systems approach.

3

Applying the New Psychology to Get Workers Interested

By 1914 Henry Ford had made two dramatic moves which, hand in hand, have formed a fundamental underlying concept with the business world ever since. Ford completed his development of the assembly line, and he proceeded to pay his assembly line workers the then unheard of figure of $5 for an eight hour day.

In effect, what Ford was saying, and what we have tacitly recognized ever since, is that:

> . . . People are most productive when they are most highly specialized—when the job is broken up into the smallest possible elements for them to accomplish;
> . . . That such work is intrinsically boring, but the boredom is necessary for the achievement of high productivity;
> . . . That the only way to continue to get productivity of the people who are trapped in such boring jobs is paying them more money.

We are so close to these concepts that we take them for granted. Look around the operation which you head. How many people are working on one coherent whole, or a chunk of the job that is large enough to contain a beginning, a middle and an end? Then, how many people are working on "small bits," or fragmented and repetitious operations? An objective look will show you a lot more fragmentation than you might have believed was the case. The assembly line does not only exist within the factory. The "assembly line concept" has become a fundamental and pervasive way of American corporate life.

And—let's face it; the idea has paid off. Over the years, "assembly line type operations," manned by experienced people who know their jobs and are willing to do them, have provided higher output than would have been the case if the work were organized in some other way. So naturally, in times of shrinking productivity, managers frequently turn to additional doses of specialization.

But somehow this *doesn't seem to work (as well) anymore*. People are different from the way they used to be. The reasons for this can be speculated upon endlessly—universal education, television, etc. These are changes in the American way of life and American values. For our purposes here, the reasons do not matter. The fact is this: increased specialization will no longer produce the payoffs in productivity that it used to do.

And more money does not seem to provide the answer. Industrial psychologists, notably Maslow and Herzberg, have been telling us that this is so and have been trying to tell us why. Herzberg says that compensation is primarily a "hygiene factor," which cannot motivate a man to do a better job.

WHY SPECIALIZATION ISN'T WORKING (AS WELL) ANY MORE

So we have a situation in which people do not respond to highly specialized tasks the way they used to—and cannot be made to like or do these tasks well by infusions of more money. Most of us do not need psychologists or management consultants to tell us that this is happening—we see it every day. Nevertheless, a good many managers simply do not know of any alternative to specialization. They see beneath them a lot of turned-off "robots" going through the motions. They bemoan the fact that there isn't more money available to "motivate" these people into doing better jobs.

It's all fallacy. There's no doubt that the supremacy of specialization is an enduring myth—but that's what it is, a myth. It looks good on paper, but work is performed by human beings who do not always conform to flow charts or mathematical models.

When you find your people are losing interest, or are becoming "turned off," what can you do? You can restructure their jobs so that they do a *greater, not a smaller, chunk of the work.*

This has been tried with interesting results. For example, Dr. Chris Argyris of Yale was able to reorganize a small electronics manufacturing department from an assembly-line procedure into a bench-assembly setup, in which each worker built an entire radio from start to finish. *There was no diminution in productivity.* There were no gains in paper output either; but the gains came in reduced turnover, lateness and absenteeism—and higher employee morale.

Theories and concepts should be re-examined as circumstances change. The assembly-line burgeoned at a time in our history when the labor force was largely made up of immigrants or first-generation Americans, with limited education, language problems, and extremely limited ideas of what they were entitled to expect out of life. That day is past; that labor force, in great part, does not exist any more. Today's worker—and this includes the "hardcore disadvantaged" black worker—simply will not respond well to long stretches of grindingly boring work.

Of course, over the past 25 years efforts have been made to overcome the problem by giving more meaning to the typical factory task. At first this concept was called "job enlargement," but that name indicates a major limitation of the approach. Mere *enlargement* of the job often led to a situation in which the worker was performing ten meaningless tasks instead of three. So nowadays we talk more about "job enrichment," which comprises a whole series of attempts to give challenge and meaningfulness to production work.

An enriched job is one from which an individual can derive

personal satisfaction and pride. He can't achieve much pride or satisfaction when he knows he is doing a job that could be performed by a mental retardate. As a matter of fact, Dr. Argyris once populated an entire factory with residents of a mental institution—with resulting increases in productivity and diminution of grievances. This is a trenchant commentary upon the kinds of jobs that industry has created for its workers.

HOW TO ENRICH THE JOBS OF YOUR SUBORDINATES

You can help to enrich the jobs of your subordinates in a wide variety of ways.

Enrichment through broadening. This is a take-off on Argyris's switching the electronics operation from assembly-line to bench-assembly. Here is how Larry Collins, the manager of the customer-service department for an equipment firm, used the concept to build creativity.

This company sells machine tools, paint sprayers, storage shelves, and industrial seating to manufacturers. The service department was organized by product line. If the customer needed service on a lathe, John Garcia made the call. If a paint spraying assembly broke down, Joe Mancini was sent. Each service man was a specialist on a particular class of equipment.

The productivity of the department was dropping. Morale was low; the servicemen, although they knew their jobs, were not "putting out." The answer: the manager switched from a specialized setup to one in which each serviceman handled all service calls for a list of companies. These were his "clients."

Of course, some restraining was necessary, but not a great deal. The servicemen liked the setup; it gave them a feeling of greater importance. And they began to do a better job.

Enrichment through "connecting-up." A worker's job can be enriched without changing the details of his job at all.

The accounts payable department of a consumer products firm was in bad shape. People seemed to work hard at their jobs, but without any zest and with low output. They were remote from the other operations of the company. They were only vaguely aware of the actual product lines. All they knew were bills, purchase orders, invoices, and open accounts.

So the manager, Carl Ferrard, decided to "connect-up" the jobs of his people with what really went on in the company. He put up displays of print advertising. He brought in other department heads to explain their outfits' functions. And Carl always pointed out the connection: "These invoices are a key part in getting our new advertising campaign in front of millions of customers for our new Crunchy-Nuts."

In a relatively short time the accounts payable people lost their sense of isolation. Now the figures they looked at were more than just numbers. An invoice clerk upped his output 300 percent. Average processing time was cut by a quarter. The saving amounted to more than $150,000 for the year.

Enrichment through variety. This happened in the home office of a nation-wide firm of sales representatives. The supervisors were complaining about the secretarial help. The secretaries complained that they were bored, the work was monotonous, and they sometimes didn't have enough to do. So Ralph Gordon, the manager, got everybody to agree to a "secretary-switching" experiment. Each secretary switched to a new boss from month to month. It did not disrupt operations; the girls kept each other briefed. At first, in the new assignments, secretaries took a little longer to handle certain things, but they had had time on their hands anyway. The secretaries responded enthusiastically to the idea of new challenges, new chores, and new bosses. The bosses liked it because they were working with more eager secretaries. The secretarial strength of the entire department was built up, because the women sharpened skills that had been getting rusty. Secretaries were better equipped to cover for each other on absences and vacations. Morale and work improved enormously. The questions we hear perhaps more than any others are: "How can I motivate my people?" "Why don't people care about their jobs?" "How can I get them to work as hard as I do?"

To the last we often answer, "Have you thought about making their jobs as interesting as the job you do?"

MAKING PEOPLE EAGER TO GET TO WORK

It is possible to build jobs that people *enjoy* doing, even to the point that they "can't wait to get in in the morning."

Visionary? No. Take the case of a man who sits all day at a bench, welding wires to terminals in TV sets. He goes home and works on the elaborate ship model he has been building for two years. The hobby does not involve enormous commitments of money or monumental decisions, but it does give the man the sense of *progression* and accomplishment that he is not getting at work. Why shouldn't his job afford him some of the same kind of kicks?

How can management begin to think in terms of job enrichment?

First, as we have said, *challenge the assumption that the present way is the only way or necessarily the best way;* it is not.

Then, *really find out what rank-and-file workers do.* For some managers it has been years since they really looked at the jobs their people perform. Sit alongside the woman who collates endless piles of paper for half an hour; you will begin to get the picture.

Concentrate on the most repetitive jobs. Frequently these are the ones in which the least capital outlay has been made for equipment. When management has spent a large sum on a machine, it devotes more thought to the mental state of the man who operates that machine. Look at the clerical jobs, the "batching" jobs—those in which an employee stays in one place and does the same thing over and over again.

Go to the supervisor and get his ideas; he is close to the scene. It may take a little while to get him to think along new lines; after all he, too, is likely to think that this is the "only way." Talk about the possibilities for building *movement* (just plain physical movement, maybe) and *progression* into the job so that the person doing it can, from time to time, get the satisfaction of accomplishment that comes from *finishing something.*

Job enrichment is a project that should not be too closely masterminded by top management. In fact, we feel that usually the best thing for management to do is determine the need, get the workers and supervisors involved—and then get out of the way. Some executives say that workers simply will not come up with any ideas at all—or that their ideas will be so outlandish as to make them impossible to execute. Our experience belies this; workers and front-line supervisors, when they know that management is thoroughly committed to the project, come up with useful and practical ways to enrich the job.

Horace Park, after racking his brains to come up with ways to introduce some liveliness into the tasks of a group of workers who did repetitive assembly work, finally gave up and put the problem to his supervisors, who in turn asked the workers. Within a week, they came back with a plan that included some controlled switching of jobs, the introduction of a contest with a modest prize, a rolling coffee and doughnut cart that would bring the worker a little refreshment at his station, and a few other ideas. A month after these recommendations were put into effect, departmental output was up 8 percent.

Deeply-embedded assumptions are hard to shake. But the idea of job enrichment is no longer a luxury item or a peripheral issue. The negative effects of job boredom are showing up heavily at the bottom line. And, if people have boring jobs to do, management has created those jobs—and management has the power to make the jobs more interesting and rewarding. Not out of altruism, but out of a concern for profit.

WHY YOU SHOULD SET "IMPOSSIBLE GOALS"

Definitions of the manager's job vary widely—but we may agree, that whatever else he does, goal-setting is one of his functions. All managers set goals for the people who report to them, either explicitly or by implication, but managers don't always realize that there is a distinct relationship between their expectations of subordinates (or at least the expectation they manifest) and how well those subordinates actually perform.

Nowadays we find a great tendency toward "soft" goal-setting. One president put it to us this way: "I try to set *reality* goals. There is no point in setting up standards that a man is not likely to be able to achieve. If people are constantly falling short, they lose morale. When one of my men does not have too much self-confidence, I try to give him targets that he can reach."

For example: Salesman Ted Walker is one of the strongest producers on the force. His volume has climbed an average of 20 percent for each of the past three years. So his manager sets the next year's quota for Walker at 23 percent higher.

Salesman Paul Varney is on a plateau. His volume has been about the same for three years. The sales manager sets a quota for Varney that is just about what the salesman has been doing.

A lot of businessmen do the same thing. They expect less of the shakily-motivated man who does not expect much from himself. And at first glance there seems to be psychological backing for this. As the work of Skinner and his followers has become popular, we have developed a strong awareness of the importance of *reinforcement*. According to this principle, the manager feels that there is little or no reward for the man who fails to meet expectations. So the logical corollary is to set the goals lower; cut the coat to fit the cloth.

There is increasingly strong evidence that this is the wrong approach.

Some fresh work being done in this area shows that *high expectancies of competence are positively related to performance.* This is true of the man who is *not* highly self-motivated—just as it is true of the individual with high self-esteem.

In other words, people are more productive when they are *striving toward high goals, even though the likelihood of achieving those goals may be remote.*

We see it in history. The great leaders, such as Churchill, Roosevelt, etc., set extremely high standards for their followers. One of the cardinal factors in the great industrial resurgence of Japan is the enormously high expectation that is set for Japanese workers by their leaders.

We believe that managers should *not* "cut the coat to fit the cloth," and that they should set up high expectations for all sub-ordinates, the low-motivated ones as well as those who brim with self-confidence.

But, we are sometimes asked, where does the reinforcement come in? The fact is, *setting of high standards is in itself a powerful form of reinforcement.* It demonstrates the confidence that the boss and the organization have in the individual. Seeing this, the low-motivated man will develop more confidence in himself.

Some intellectuals scorn this concept. They feel strongly that it is against the humanist tradition to expect more from a man than he seems able to give. We disagree. The manager's job is to make people more productive, and the setting of high expectation is a fair and legitimate way of doing this.

The manager who sets high goals for all of his people cannot, however, just let it go at that. If a worker, contemplating the expectations that his superior manifests, is beset with fear that he will be penalized or fired for not achieving the goals, then the result is the opposite of reinforcement. So the good executive places a safety net under his low-motivated people. He makes it clear that he believes the objectives are capable of being achieved, but he is there with help and counsel if the subordinate seems to be falling far short.

Let's say the sales manager sets a high goal for his plateau-bound performer, Paul Varney. The sales manager is obligated to spend some time with Varney, advising him, counseling him, shoring up his ego. But the added expenditure of time is apt to be more than repaid by better performance.

Obviously, when goals are set high, there is a greater chance that many of them will not be met. But the manager's function is not to give everyone a target that he can hit. It is to make everyone as productive as possible, and this can best be done through the setting of *motivational* expectations rather than "reality" goals.

1. *Set high goals for all of your people.*
2. *Be ready to help those who seem to be falling short of goals.*

3. Continue to set high standards even though people may fall short of them.

HOW TO TALK TO PEOPLE IN A WAY
THAT REALLY GETS THROUGH TO THEM

We've been taught about "the power of positive thinking." We've heard all about "how to win friends and influence people." There has been so much positiveness and winning of friends, that many managers feel it to be a mortal sin to say "no" to anybody. Current management wisdom seems to imply that one must never utter a discouraging word.

We beg to differ. We would like to talk about the power of *negative talking*.

If you were suddenly asked to say which of the Ten Commandments comes first to your mind, what would you reply? Most people would respond by saying "Thou shalt not kill"; or "Thou shalt not steal"; or even "Thou shalt not commit adultery." Few would reply, "I am the Lord thy God . . . Thou shalt have no other Gods before Me"; or "Honor thy father and thy mother."

We remember the *specific negative prohibitions* rather than the broad positive injunctions. The fact that our minds work this way has a bearing for managers on the handling of problem people.

We were talking with the president of a sporting goods company about one of his key executives. The president said, "He is a talented guy; but sometimes he is such a louse that I believe he creates more headaches than he is worth. He is touchy, and emotional, and insulting. He is sarcastic and abrasive. And he keeps on interfering in other departments where he has no business interfering."

The subject of our conversation is a gifted manager, whose absence would be sorely felt. So, we asked, what was the president doing to help him to get straightened out. "Well," said the president, "I've talked to him. Of course, I try to keep the thing on a positive level. I have emphasized his good points, and try to make it clear to him what I would like him to be. To be a really top-notch executive he should be understanding, tactful, calm, unabrasive. And when we talk he agrees with me. But then he goes out and does the same things all over again."

Influenced by the hundreds of thousands of words that have been written and spoken on "human relations," and by his own natural distaste for "treating people like they were children," the president has been *accentuating the positive*. And, as often happens, it *doesn't seem to work*. The interview is dignified; the culprit agrees 100 percent, but he keeps on doing the things that have loused him up.

Positive thinking has been carried too far. In cases like this, a small dose of *negative thinking* would be more effective. We suggested to the president that, instead of concentrating on the qualities he would like his subordinate to possess—the DO's— he instead issue a list of DON'T's. They might run something like this:

. . . "Don't insult people publicly. If you want to complain to me about a man, okay; but don't tell him what's wrong with him to his face";

. . . "Don't keep telling people how good your department is";

. . . "Don't bang on the table at meetings. You may articulate your points as strongly as you want—but don't bang on the table";

. . . "Don't tell other people how to run their departments";

. . . "Don't call meetings of your people at nine p.m. after they have been working all day";

. . . "Don't talk to anyone when you know you have a chip on your shoulder."

At first the president cringed at the notion. After all, wasn't this treating a grown man like a child? But the other approach had not worked; and so he decided to give our suggestions a try. *It seems to be paying off.* The "wild man" subordinate took it better than the president had dared hope. Furthermore, the problem manager appears to have taken at least some of these negative injunctions to heart. He is operating less abrasively.

Why? Specific "don'ts" are easier to remember and act upon than glowing "do's." The broad exhortation to be good is fine, but we tend to see it as something beyond our reach. But if we are told, "Thou shalt not be rude," or "Thou shalt not sneer at thy neighbor," then we have something that can be grasped and acted upon.

There is a sound reason for the greater effectiveness of the negative prohibition as against the positive exhortation. This reason resides in the difference between *attitude* and *behavior*. When we talk generalities to a man, we are hoping to modify his *attitudes*. It is very easy for a man to agree that a certain attitude is laudable and worthy of his adoption—but it is very hard for him to put this agreement into practice. However, when he is told to stop *behaving* in a certain specific way—this he can grasp, and do something about. Furthermore, psychologists have discovered that, in certain instances, the *only* way to ultimately change a man's attitude is by modifying his behavior.

Dale Carnegie's methods were successful, not because he issued pious platitudes, but because he offered precise prohibitions. A great deal of winning friends and influencing people consisted simply in observing some easily understood taboos . . . like, (although Mr. Carnegie never put it this way) "Thou shalt not shoot thy mouth off when the other guy wants to talk."

We are not suggesting the abolition of positive precepts, or that the Ten Commandments be rewritten into a "Decalogue of Don'ts." But we do suggest that specific undesirable behavior can often be changed more readily by saying "Thou shalt *not*. . ." rather than saying "Thou shall." For example, take the employee who is frequently late. You can try the positive approach. . . "Len, it makes it tougher on everybody when some one is not on time, so I know that you will make every effort to be onhand. . ." But you'll do better with the negative: "Len, *don't be late*."

Do people resent the negative approach? Not nearly as much as a lot of managers fear. As a matter of fact, many workers welcome negatives; they are clear and easy to remember.

When you want someone to stop doing something, don't try to be long-winded and circuitous for the sake of being "popular." Tell him clearly and distinctly not to do it; and tell him what the penalty is if he continues to do it.

THE NEW ART OF THE 30-MINUTE MEETING

We are talking about ways to get workers interested. In practical terms, the manager often interests his people to the extent that he eliminates those things which turn them off. If people are bored stiff with certain of the day-in, day-out aspects of their jobs, they are simply not going to respond to any amount of motivational effort. You cannot get them interested.

We have talked about how some of the lower level rote jobs in your operations can be enriched and made more interesting without loss of productivity. What about the people higher up in the scale—those key people on whom you rely for supervision and policy? How bored are they getting, and what bores them?

Repetition and redundancy bore people, and one of the most insidious conduits of boredom is often the department meeting. Meetings are necessary and useful, but when regular meetings have been going over an extended period of time, with pretty much the same cast of characters, the whole procedure becomes overlaid with ceremonious elements of irrelevancy and boredom.

What about your meetings? Is the same meeting always held at the same time? Do the same people always come? Is the same or similar subject matter usually covered? How long do the meetings last? More than an hour? If the answer is yes, more than an hour, it may well be that you have on your hands not only a virulent time waster, but also a lethally boring procedure. If you suspect that this is the case, you can accomplish a great deal toward reinteresting your people by doing something about your meeting structure.

1. *Eliminate all the routine.* Many recurring meetings begin with routine matters which are disposed of before fresh material is even considered. This is psychologically and motiva-

tionally wrong. Think about starting your next meeting by saying, "Unless anyone objects, let's dispense with the routine opening and go right to something new. Who has a fresh idea?"

If the routine material is really necessary, and the meeting is really the most effective way of disseminating it, *hold it for the end*. Use the beginning of the meeting when people are "up" to try to get your most creative efforts.

2. *Rotate chairmanship of the meeting.* Do you always run the meeting? Let someone else run it. This is not, after all, a diminution of your authority. The fact is that running is often a mechanical chore from which the manager should be freed. If he does not have to worry about calling upon speakers, writing things on charts, etc., he is better able to evaluate and contribute to what is being said.

3. *On occasion, cut out the meeting altogether.* One manager works it this way. People show up for the meeting; he writes a brief description of a problem on a chart or blackboard before the group, and then he says, "Let's not discuss this right away. Instead, let's everybody go right back to his office and just sit and think about it for 15 minutes. *Then* we'll reconvene and see what contributions we have."

Once you begin taking a look at the meetings you hold with an objective eye, you will see many ways in which much of the nonsense can be cut, in order to make for shorter sessions and far less boredom. The fact is, you can even make meetings interesting again.

A NEW AND IMPROVED VERSION OF BRAINSTORMING

It's a brainstorming meeting. The manager sets the groundrules: "Okay. The thing is to pop out as many ideas as possible—no criticism, no negative thinking. If you want to add to the other fellow's idea, 'hitchhike' on it. The subject is how to sell the new Model 5000. Let's go."

A short pause. Then it starts:

"Advertise it on TV."
"Introduce it at a big meeting in Bermuda."

"Make a lottery out of it. Each buyer gets a number, and there are periodic drawings."

"Hitchhike. Make the prizes indefinite service contracts."

And so it goes. Many of the ideas are fantastic. Some are "in the ballpark." And a few may even be practical.

About twenty years ago, Alex Osborne's "brainstorming" was a new business rage. After all, a brainstorming meeting was simple to conduct. All you needed was a room, a few people, and the reiterated reminder, "no criticism." We don't hear much about brainstorming today. Why? Well, brainstorming turned out to be not quite as simple as it looked. Few managers knew how to make a brainstorming meeting pay off. The sessions were lively—but the crop of really useful ideas was distressingly thin. The people who attended the meetings, noting the disappointing pay-off, began to lose interest. And so the brainstorming meeting subsided from view.

But some behavioral scientists refused to give up on the technique. They admitted the flaws, but insisted that the basic idea of brainstorming was sound. Now we present a revised and updated concept of brainstorming, which you can use to "turn on" key people and to generate creative ideas.

Some interesting sidelights on brainstorming have been provided by Drs. Panayiota A. Collaros and Lynn R. Anderson of Wayne State University. These psychologists conducted experiments bearing on one of the essential assumptions of brainstorming: that participants will vie with each other in producing novel ideas in a completely uninhibited fashion.

The subjects of this study were divided into three groups of 80 persons each. Each group was broken up into small segments for the purpose of brainstorming.

In Group I, each participant was given instructions containing this paragraph:

Read this carefully, as you are the only person in this group who has not participated in a brainstorming session before. All other members are familiar with the procedure to be followed.

Group II got a different paragraph:

Only one person has participated in a brainstorming session before. The rest should read the following very carefully to become familiar with the procedure to be followed.

Group III received sheets containing no comments at all about the experience of other members of the meetings.

Group I, supposedly "loaded" with experts, conducted highly-inhibited meetings at which relatively little in the way of productive creativity was accomplished. Their ideas were sparse and commonplace. Group II, with one "expert" to each meeting, did better. Group III, in which there was no information about the experience of participants, did best.

In talking to the subjects afterward, Drs. Collaros and Anderson found that many individuals were quite hesitant to offer "far-out" ideas because they feared the disapproval and unvoiced criticism of those who were more experienced. The psychologists concluded, "Overall, the results of the study indicate that social factors inherent in unequal status structures within the group are detrimental to member creativity even though brainstorming instructions are given. Group members feel threatened and inhibited by the presence of more knowledgeable members. . . This finding may explain, in part, why many studies which have compared the creativity of individuals who are brainstorming alone and in groups unanimously endorse the superiority of the 'alone' condition."

You can tell a man that he need not be inhibited, but if he feels that the others around the table draw more water than he does, he *will* be inhibited. He will "self-weight" his own contributions before offering them, and this is the antithesis of brainstorming.

Does the thrust of these experiences and findings completely discredit brainstorming as a technique? In our judgment, it does not.

By and large, we maintain that the individual approach to problems will work better and more economically than the group approach. But sameness leads to boredom. Every manager who is trying to elicit creative thinking from his staff will welcome an occasional change of pace. Once in a while, a brainstorming session can be productive, if it is conducted according to these principles:

1. Concentrate the discussion in a *narrow subject area*. Permit no broad dissertations and digressions.

2. Rule out *all logical judgment*. Don't halt the flow of ideas by stopping to criticize or evaluate.

3. Welcome *free-association*. The wilder the ideas, the better.

4. Encourage *hitchhiking*. When one man comes up with a wild notion, another man should try to make the same notion even wilder.

5. Demand *quantity*. The more ideas you get, the better the chance of coming up with some you can use.

6. Seek *improvement* and *combination*. Take parts of two ideas and join them for a third.

And above all, give a great deal of thought to the "mix" of the group. As Drs. Collaros and Anderson suggest, "careful attention should be given to the selection of members for the brainstorming group by making previous experience as similar as possible." And, if there are great differences within the group, do everything you can to *minimize* these differences.

THE SPECIAL CASE--MANAGING CREATIVE PEOPLE

What we have said about getting people interested applies to a great majority of those who report to you. These are the average, near-average, little-better-than-average performers who—let's face it—constitute the backbone of most departments and most companies. No troop is made up of 100% stars. If you are able to "turn on" the people of reasonable competency who work for you, you will be accomplishing one of the fundamental tasks of management.

However, every operation contains, or certainly *should* contain, exceptional performers. We mean those creative people, often with oddball traits, who often provide the most dramatic solutions to the biggest problems.

Some managers are frightened of creative people. They don't understand them; they don't know how to handle them; they think the operation would be better off without them. Not so; without the *creative exception,* most operations can't rise to the heights. And you should want to rise to the heights—at least once in a while. Not only is it exhilarating, it sometimes is just plain necessary.

How can creative people, such as those in advertising, merchandising, design, and R&D be managed for maximum effect? Obviously, they cannot be exempted from all rules and regulations. It is equally obvious they require a certain special touch in management.

It can be done. Here are twelve rules for getting top performance out of creative people.

These rules are keyed to one overriding principle—supervision is the critical factor. *The creative man's relationship with his superior overshadows every other influence.*

1. *Gear pressure to goals*

One manager puts it this way: many creative people "need the reassurance of gentle pressure on the reins." Not steady pressure—an occasional touch.

For the creative man often works best in fits and starts. He needs latitude. He chafes under constant scrutiny. But he will respond to the occasional touch that reminds him of his objective.

2. *Maintain contact*

As Dr. Donald Pelz of Michigan University remarks, "Creative performance is highest when supervision provides an *intermediate* degree of independence."—not total, "you're on your own," independence. For some people this is just the ticket, but the creative man should not be allowed to lose contact with his superior. He benefits from knowing that there is a sympathetic ear available to him.

Frequent communication, coupled with freedom to make certain decisions, seems the best compromise.

3. Let him know where he stands

The creative man, more than most, hungers for evaluation of his efforts. But appraisal is difficult. It is probably futile to evaluate his procedures, and results may be a long time in coming.

Under these circumstances, the creator may feel a letdown.

. . . He may not complain, but watch for signs of brooding resentment;

. . . Talk informally with your people; demonstrate continuing interest in their problems;

. . . Redefine objectives frequently; show that you know what each individual is seeking;

. . . When results come, be openhanded in demonstrating that you know their importance;

. . . Pass along the reactions of others in management.

4. Give him ample time alone

For many of us, it goes against the grain to see an employee sitting with his feet propped up, staring into nothingness. We are inclined to urge that he relax on his own time. But this is when many of the brightest ideas occur to him.

This point may seem to conflict with #2—*Maintain contact;* but it does not really. The idea is to let the creative man know that the contact is there and available to him, but leave him alone.

This is not to suggest that creative men invariably wish to, or should, work in seclusion. Sometimes several scientists coming together *after* individual study stimulate each other, and accomplish more at that stage than they would individually.

But let them choose the time to be alone and the time to congregate.

5. *Make him secure*

An idea man needs challenge. But he responds best when his *mind* is challenged—not his self or his security. His self-confidence, often vulnerable, is his protective shield for the sensitive and difficult mental mechanisms.

"No creative individual," said the late Dr. Edwin Tolman, "can function well when he is too frightened, too insecure, too emotional, or too anything else."

So it is important to help the creator to build and preserve his self-confidence. Pay him well; give him security and satisfaction in the job; and grant any reasonable requests that he may make.

6. *Be willing to tolerate failure*

We all learned, as children, about the number of times great thinkers and great men met defeat before they won through . . . "if at first you don't succeed," etc. But it's a little different when a man is failing while he is on our payroll. We feel a nudge toward impatience.

But a creative atmosphere requires that a man be able to present radical, even unworkable ideas without being harshly judged. (Your company's leading product may have sounded like a gag when it was first proposed.)

All ideas are not good ideas. When you ask a man to experiment, innovate and create, you must accept the idea that you are giving him a greater margin for error than you allow to others in more predictable occupations. And you must let him know this, by word, deed and attitude. If you don't, fear of failure will stifle true initiative—and whatever you are paying for it is blown.

7. *Respect his outside sources of stimulation*

As we have noted, the creator is often oriented toward his profession rather than his company. This may clash with some of our ideas about loyalty, but it is a fact that must be faced.

Thus the scientist tends to spend a lot of time on non-company activities with non-company people—professional societies, conventions, academic gatherings, and lectures or articles for specialized groups. He needs these things to refresh himself, and he needs the ego-building identification with an elite that transcends business.

Some companies discourage such activities, but this is shortsighted. More and more these days, we must accept the idea that gifted people cannot find full satisfaction within the company.

8. *Provide a creative atmosphere*

Men do not produce ideas when they are uncomfortable. Creative people grow uncomfortable and unhappy in an environment of "by-the-book" procedure and (to them) pointless drudgery.

It makes sense to relieve creators of routine chores—the filling out of certain kinds of reports, for example. Also, consider the physical setup. Quiet, comfort and convenience may not be essential to productive thought, but they can help it along. Attractive secretaries have also been known to help.

9. *Recognize creativity*

Creative people like to think that they are "special." This can rankle, as others then say, "Who the hell does he think he is?"

But if you are paying a man to think, you might as well offer the kind of recognition that will help to stimulate thought. So, recognize creativity as something special.

For example, in an engineering department of Eastman Kodak, management has taken several steps to acknowledge the "special" status of the creative engineers:

. . . The salary structure recognizes different levels of creative performance;

. . . Unusual achievements are well publicized;

. . . Individuals are encouraged to talk about achievements to their peers in professional and technical organizations;

. . . Engineers are encouraged to obtain professional licenses and display them where they work.

10. *Don't demand total creativity*

You can't expect a man to be firing off ideas like popcorn every moment of the day. In fact, a 100% creative man, with *no* other attributes, is not likely to be an asset.

The man with something else to offer will work out better in a business organization, even if he is slightly less cerebral than the "pure thinker." David Ogilvy made the point well: "It is usually useless to be wholly creative. In addition to being an original thinker, you must be able to sell what you create. Management cannot be expected to recognize a good idea unless it is presented by a good salesman." You are justified and wise to require, at least, that the creator be able to convey his ideas clearly.

11. *Evaluate the creative product quickly*

Executives may be impatient, but creators are even more impatient. They like—and need—to have their contributions evaluated quickly, and to get fast feedback. When a man is waiting "for the other shoe to drop," he is not thinking.

Of course, premature disclosure on an idea may be unfortunate—even dangerous. Take the necessary time to contemplate the creative man's suggestion (and no more time than necessary), but, meanwhile, feed back to him so that he knows you are working on it.

12. *Don't deny creators their innocent and harmless foibles*

It costs little or nothing to overlook oddities, and it pays off, because they might just be essential to creative functioning. We know one excellent writer who cannot write a word until he places a full pitcher of ice water next to his typewriter—no glass, just a pitcher. Schiller, the great German poet and playwright, was stimulated by the smell of apples rotting inside his desk. Freud felt that he could not think without a cigar in his mouth.

Such harmless quirks are known to psychologists as sensory stimulants; they "cue in" the creator's idea mechanism. If they cause no disturbance, get used to them and encourage others to do the same.

Thoreau said it, and it's good advice: "If a man does not keep pace with his companions, perhaps it is because he hears a different drummer. Let him step to the music which he hears, however measured or far away."

A PLAN FOR GETTING PEOPLE INTERESTED

Make jobs interesting by giving people "more of the whole" to do.

Set goals high—and keep them high.

When necessary, get tough. It breaks through emotional blocks and gets people interested.

Shake up routine functions, such as meetings. Try a new way of brainstorming.

Keep creative people "turned on" by handling them intelligently—but not gingerly.

4

Using New Psychological Methods to Keep People Producing

Momentum is a key word in sports—and in business too. It's important to get people to a satisfactory level of effort; and it's equally important to keep them there. Here are some recently uncovered suggestions and techniques for maintaining that all-important momentum in your workers.

HOW TO MAKE ENERGY CURVES WORK FOR YOU

Every manager has noted that different subordinates seem to be at their best at different points in the day. Smith may be "up" early in the morning; this is when he is at his brightest and gets most work done. Jones, on the other hand, doesn't seem to really get going until later in the afternoon. When you talk with him in the morning, you don't seem to really get through to him. He often says "I'll get to it later today," and usually he does. He is the fellow who is around the place after everyone else has gone home. To take another case, Brown may be at his best around the middle of the day. When everyone else goes to lunch, he grabs a sandwich at his desk and works on something.

To a lot of managers, this is annoying. They try to get everybody's working habits into harmony, but their efforts don't seem

77

to be effective. In the morning, before he is really ready for this, the manager finds Smith at his door, full of bright ideas. With Jones, however, he can't really seem to have much in the way of fruitful discussion, because Jones is doing most of his thinking late in the day or in the evening. Brown too, can be a headache. The manager says, "Let's go out and get some lunch and I'll tell you my ideas on this." And Brown replies, "Well, I'm working on that report, and I was figuring on eating in so I can get it finished by this afternoon."

The manager's job is to get work out of these people, all of whom seem to have diverse quirks about when they function best. Some managers fight hard to push their people into operating into some kind of "decent" standard of production during a "normal" day. This can be a costly and time-consuming mistake, because what is "normal" for THE MANAGER MAY NOT BE NORMAL FOR HIS PEOPLE.

The reason for this, as scientists are discovering (or rediscovering), is that each of us operates on his own individual *energy curve*.

In understanding why workers have high and low points during the day and in doing something about them, it is extremely useful to be familiar with the concept of "circadian rhythms" (from the Latin circa dies, "around a day"). Each of us has a circadian rhythm which functions as an internal clock . . . "within each day many of our physiological functions undergo fluctuations as large as 70 degrees." It is not important here for us to go very deeply into the physiological basis for the concept of daily rhythm. The hormones lie at the center of it. Executives who travel a lot have experienced this phenomenon most dramatically in terms of "jet fatigue"—the lingering disorientation and exhaustion that sets in when we travel fast to another place a considerable distance away.

However, these rhythms operate all the time, on a mundane, everyday level. They operate on all of us, and this leads to one of the big difficulties in getting productive work out of people. For many managers are not aware that they are operating on a curve. The manager has a general feeling that he is more "with it" at a certain time, say early in the morning. He assumes that this is the norm, and he expects that those who work with him will conform to that norm. The manager may not always do this knowingly, but his assumption that his own rhythm is the norm underlies his efforts to motivate and work with the people who report to him. Thus he may frequently be trying to force people into a pattern which is not right for them. In doing this, he is struggling against a natural process, rather than going with it. This can result in constant unhappiness and frustration in efforts to get the most out of subordinates.

Take the case of a manager who likes to handle routine functions like correspondence early in the day. He tends to schedule meetings later in the morning and over lunch. He prefers to take on the more creative and demanding aspects of his job, such as planning and decision-making, in the afternoon. Of course he is involved with subordinates during each phase of his day. He may find one subordinate, ostensibly an experienced and capable man, who always seems "out of phase." The manager may conclude of this subordinate that "it is all in his head." These new findings in the behavioral sciences tell us that it is *not* "all in his head." If the manager is to work with this subordinate in a truly productive fashion, he must approach the problem differently.

So it is vital for you to understand how the individual energy curve works. Let's consider it.

WHY PEOPLE CAN DO MORE UNDER STRESS

Most of us are aware that, at moments of sudden stress or extreme danger, something happens to our blood. You are crossing the street, thinking of this and that. Suddenly, from behind you comes the loud blare of a horn and the squeal of brakes. What happens? *You move fast*. You make a broad jump that, under normal circumstances, you would never be capable of. A moment later you feel weak and depleted. What has occurred is that a lightning charge of energy has been exploded inside you by the instantaneous action of the adrenal glands, which, acting on the signal from the brain, have pumped the hormones ACTH and adrenalin into the bloodstream. The adrenalin releases a rich burst of sugar from the liver. The pituitary and thyroid glands are activated; other functions are switched to "maximum voltage" —and all within the fraction of a second.

The emergency produces a massive, life-saving bodily reaction. In the prehistoric dawn of man's existence upon earth, dangers were ever present. The protective glandular mechanism was called upon often to respond to instant peril. Nowadays, under normal conditions of civilization, this phenomenon takes place only rarely. But this does not mean that the adrenal glands are inoperative. The fact is that they are frequently at work, discharging small amounts of stress hormones into the bloodstream in response to the stresses of everyday life. We become irritated at a colleague; we experience a sudden twinge of worry about the state of the economy and how it is affecting our security; we engage in a domestic run-in with one of the children over schoolwork, hair, dress, or use of the car. Each time, our blood receives a hormonal charge.

Physiologists have learned more. They have learned that the glands work minutely, but steadily, throughout the day and night. And the secretion of stress hormones operates on a curve. Dr. Seymour N. Farber, Dean of Educational Services and Director of Continuing Education in Health Sciences at the University of California's San Francisco Medical Center, is a widely-recognized authority on stress, particularly the kind of stress to which executives are prone. He has described for us experiments in which blood samples were taken from subjects at various hours of the day and tested for hormone content. Dr. Farber traces the curve . . . "in the dawn hours, the curve of these stress hormones, which gives you powers of resistance, is at the lowest. As it rises, it is near the hour of eleven o'clock, or at noontime, that it reaches its peak and we are forceful, creative and attentive. . . During the afternoon, the curve goes down, and about five or six o'clock, again you do not have hormonal strength of resistance; you are not at your best. At eleven o'clock in the evening, it rises again, not to the level of noontime (but high enough to explain the population explosion).''

Dr. Farber goes on to point out several ways in which we may work *against* what is going on inside us:

. . . "Let us compare the hormone curve with our daily lives. Too often we get up in the morning with very little resistance (and this is also true of the wife) and, after an argument, away to work we go, and take it out on the first associate we see at the job."

Now Dr. Farber discusses one of the great ceremonial institutions of the executive day—*lunch*. We have always looked upon lunch as being one of the most welcome refinements of modern life. Over a cocktail and a good meal, we can relax with congenial companions, talk out our troubles and our hopes, maybe even do a little business. While Dr. Farber has nothing against the business lunch *per se,* he suggests that perhaps the traditional timing is out of phase with the hormone curve. . . "At noontime when we can best work, we take two or three martinis, we eat heavily—and we have dulled that creative drive. Actually, if we followed this physiological curve, we shouldn't eat until about two or three in the afternoon, but continue working right straight through to that time."

The American Indians, Dr. Farber suggest, were superb physiologists. He quotes their precept: "Attack the white man an hour before dawn when his courage is at the lowest ebb." (Scott Fitzgerald wrote that in the "dark night of the soul it is always three o'clock in the morning, day after day.")

Unfortunately, we sometimes fight against our hormonal curve as if occasional dips in energy were somehow unmanly, a sign of weakness. We might be much more productive managers if we were to recognize the inevitable course of these daily physiological ups and downs—and adjust to them. This takes some insight and self-inspection. When you know that at certain times during the day you feel good and capable of tackling difficult tasks, see to it that your most creative work (whenever possible) is centered around those times. Conversely, save routine work for the low periods. This may require some breaks with the traditional ways of doing things. For example, a good many of us might get a lot more done if we followed Dr. Farber's advice and delayed lunch until three in the afternoon. At first we might feel a little self-conscious about it—after all, "everybody" eats in the middle of the day. But the feeling of being a little different soon passes, and the satisfaction of greater productivity and sense of well-being more than make up for it.

Certain functions of our minds and our bodies run on pro-grammed courses that are not susceptible to much modification, no matter how hard we may try. This being the case, it makes sense for us to cooperate with our internal curves rather than make the futile effort to struggle against them.

HOW TO KEEP UP MOMENTUM—SIX BASIC STEPS

Here are the basic steps in using the concept of circadian rhythm to keep up momentum and make your department a more productive one.

1. Determine your own energy curve. Chart your own high and low points during the day.
2. Through observation, compare your curve with that of others. Don't assume that yours is the norm.
3. Form a general idea of the energy curves of your key subordinates.
4. Modify your interactions with these key subordinates to take their energy curves into account. Try to present them with the most challenging problems at times when they are most ready to handle them.
5. Encourage subordinates to understand the concept of the energy curve and to structure, within reason, their own daily schedules more systematically.
6. Continue to understand and allow for the fact that every-

body in your department is operating on his own individual energy curve.

HOW TO GET IMMEDIATE COOPERATION AND MAXIMUM EFFORT ON A NEW PROJECT

When you introduce your people to a new project, you are talking about *change*. Change can be stimulating. It can also be threatening. To win the fullest enthusiasm and cooperation from your staff, you will want to maximize the positive stimulation and minimize the threat.

Three things are important for the manager in this situation: personal enthusiasm, effective communication, and selective job structuring.

You must, first of all, radiate your own enthusiasm and confidence that the job will get done and get done well. Unfortunately, management enthusiasm, to a great degree, has gone out of style. Fifty years ago, Sinclair Lewis made "babbittry" an ignominious household word. A new breed of scientific managers grew up feeling that it was babbittry to show too much enthusiasm for the job or for some particular aspect of it. Such enthusiasm was identified with simple-minded pep talks and naive optimism.

But recent observation indicates that we have gone much too far in dispelling enthusiasm from the executive suite. Today's average worker is not going to display much zest for his job—at least overtly. If he does, he is looked at askance by his colleagues. Others think there is something odd about him. Nevertheless, many people like their jobs, or at least they *want* to like them. They look to the manager for a cue. If the manager conducts himself like a dispassionate robot, then the worker is likely to conclude that perhaps there really is something wrong with getting all "revved up," or that the job is not something to get all that excited about. It is up to the manager to provide the cue for enthusiasm in a useful and systematic fashion.

So the executive must strike a balance between winning active cooperation and maintaining control of what is going on. Here are six guidelines to follow in accomplishing this:

1. Disseminate *full* information about the new project or assignment. Without endangering security, take the risk of giving out too much information rather than too little.

2. Show how the project ties in with the overall goals and health of the company. When people know only about their finite, limited departmental goals, they are working in a vacuum. Take, for example, the situation in which the manager of an accounting department is trying to get his people to speed up certain transactions. Experience tells us that he will achieve better success if he emphasizes how this speeded up process will affect sales, production, customer relations, etc.—the other major (and sometimes more "glamorous") undertakings of the company.

3. Talk to each key subordinate about his particular part of the new responsibility. Depending upon the individual, leave more or less leeway within which the subordinate can structure his job to reach the new goal, but make sure he has a structure and that he understands it.

4. Manifest your own enthusiasm. Make it clear that you feel the overall objective is a demanding and worthy one, but that you have every confidence in the ability of the department to meet it.

5. Set up short range goals for each individual. These should be goals that are reached fairly quickly and that are easily seen.

6. Heighten contacts and interaction with subordinates during the time that a new project is getting underway. Talk to people. Find out what problems they are running into. Help them straighten out those problems. Pat them on the back for accomplishment. Make it clear to everyone that you are involved and doing your share.

HOW TO ELIMINATE DEMOTIVATING FACTORS THAT KEEP PEOPLE FROM DOING THEIR BEST

For years it has been a common complaint among managers that people just don't care. Lateness, absenteeism, sloppy workmanship, a "let George do it" approach—these are the earmarks of demotivation. It's the most natural thing in the world for a frustrated manager to determine to get rid of people who manifest such negative attitudes. But often this approach accomplishes nothing. New people come in, but they are equally lackadaisical.

The real answer may be that there are certain "demotivators" that are built into the job. These built-in demotivators are what cause initially enthusiastic workers to lose their drive, and to sluff off to the point that they are just going through the motions.

Industrial psychologists have recently been conducting a lot of research into what demotivates people, and what the manager can do about it. Here, we present eight principal areas of demotivation, along with indications of telltale clues that you can use to spot the demotivator. When one of your people is working under one or more of the adverse conditions listed here, there is good reason for him to be "turned off."

1. *Lack of clear job objectives.* When people do not know what is expected of them, or when they do not have clear standards of performance, work slacks off. Some of the clues of this condition are:

> lack of respect for supervisors,
> alibis beginning "nobody told me. . .",
> backtracking and duplication of effort,
> arguments over procedures,
> seemingly pointless questions about what to do next.

Sit down and consider each individual and each job. Clarify for yourself the standards and expectations. Then communicate standards and expectations to your workers.

2. *Standards that are set too high.* When people consistently fall short of targets because they are too far away, they become frustrated and disillusioned. Here are some of the indications of this condition:

> expressions of "what's the difference?" attitudes,
> ignoring of quality standards,
> lack of willingness to cooperate with others,

annoyed reactions to requests,
cover-up of mistakes.

Take another look at your operational standards. There may be no need to revise long range goals; but make sure that everybody has shorter range sub-goals he can accomplish within a reasonable length of time.

3. *Overly loose discipline.* When certain regulations are not enforced, or enforced spottily, the result is often a general contempt for policy and procedure. Some of the clues:

mishandling of equipment,
too much horsing around,
frequent errors of omission,
heavy lateness and absenteeism,
slovenliness on detail.

Review the rules. If some regulations are unenforceable, drop them. Let everybody know, by word and example, that the remaining rules will be enforced fairly and consistently.

4. *Too much pressure from the top.* Workers who feel that someone is constantly "riding herd" on them become demotivated and ineffective. Some of the ways you can tell this is happening:

frequent complaints about the workload,
inordinate requests for transfer,
undue moving around and restlessness on the job,
tense flare-ups between people,
irritation at new assignments.

If this is the problem, it is not necessary to relax standards, but it may be a good idea for the manager to become less omnipresent. The manager should delegate more where it is appropriate. Where additional delegation is not a good idea, he should make it a point to at least permit workers to express themselves to him.

5. *Inadequate contact with management.* When people do not have sufficient contact with or access to the boss, they begin to

get the feeling that no one higher up in the company really cares about them. You may detect this demotivator if you see these signs:

few workers come to see you,
management instructions seem to be deliberately misunderstood,
people are sarcastic or derisive about the job,
rumors and gossip flourish,
subordinates by-pass you.

Show a greater concern for the problems and interests of people—on and off the job. Go to them. Find out how they are doing. Give the feeling that you are interested and that you care.

6. *Overly heavy criticism*. Criticism—even constructive criticism—can erode the will to produce if it is not sufficiently balanced on the positive side. Some of the indications:

"rulebook" operation,
evasiveness in talking with the manager,
failure to "level" about problems and progress,
high irritability,
tense attitudes.

Review your praise quotient. Have you been looking for opportunities to pat people on the back when they do well? Make opportunities; make sure that other people in the company know about it when you applaud a job well done. Balance off criticism —not with jokes or phoney reassurance, but with constructive suggestions and offers to help.

7. *Inadequate conditions or equipment*. People particularly resent what they consider to be handicaps imposed upon them because of the company's cheapness or indifference to their working conditions. Some of the ways you can tell this is the situation:

frequent complaints,
observations that people in other departments have it better,
unforeseen foul-ups and delays,
carelessness about equipment and materials,

failure to make necessary minor adjustments,
frequent calls for repair or consultation.

Take an inventory of equipment and conditions in your operation from top to bottom. Compare with similar situations inside and outside the company. If changes are necessary, and if you have to make a fight of it up the line, be sure that your people know you are making that fight.

8. *Abdication of the leadership role.* Workers want leadership. When the manager does not provide it, there will be problems, as indicated by these clues:

emergence of informal leaders,
arguments about privileges and prerogatives,
formation of cliques,
failure to respect authority,
"forgetting" the manager's instructions or comments,
strong resistance to change.

When you see this kind of thing happening, reinstate your leadership role—not by proclaiming it, but by exemplifying it. Set objectives; make sure they are clear to everybody; then get out ahead in driving toward their accomplishment.

These are the basic demotivators that can creep into any job situation. Look for the signs, spot the demotivator and then take action to correct it.

DELEGATING WITH MINIMUM DANGER
AND MAXIMUM RESULTS

Prudent delegation is one of the keys to effective management. Every manager knows this, but most managers also realize that while it is easy to pay tributes to delegation, it is not always easy to delegate properly. The manager bears the overall responsibility and authority for attaining certain corporate objectives. In delegation, he assigns to a subordinate the authority to get certain parts of the job done. Of course, the subordinate also assumes responsibility at the same time, but this does not lighten the load of responsibility that remains upon the manager's shoulders.

Let's face it—in matters that concern our jobs, our careers, or our livelihood, it is not always easy to turn responsibility over to somebody else. If he fails, we fail too. This is one consideration that keeps managers from delegating to the degree that they should.

When we consider the subordinate on the receiving end of the delegation process, we can see another reason why many people consider delegation to be a delicate and perilous operation. A man is called in to the manager's office. The manager says "I'm turning this over to you. You're on your own." The delegatee may not feel that he has been given sufficient information about the project. He may not feel that his authority is broad enough. There may be certain details that are unclear to him. Indeed, he may not believe that he is ready to handle such an assignment on his own. But what is he going to do? He is concerned about his own progress and his own career. He wants to move ahead and make good. Too many reservations or too much nit-picking about the assignment may give the boss the idea that he is not really eager, or that he does not wish to get ahead.

Nevertheless, as we have seen, delegation is vital not only because the manager cannot do everything himself, but because it is essential to delegate to certain key subordinates, in order to motivate them and give them scope in which to grow.

There is a simple, modified approach to delegation which can go a long way toward overcoming these obstacles. We call it the "fail-safe" method of delegation. Here are the steps involved:

1. *Choose your delegatee* without letting him know at first that he has been chosen. Observe not only his experience and familiarity with the job, but also his drive, ambition and ego strength. That last point, ego strength, is important. A subordinate may have all the requisite knowledge and tools, but it takes a certain inner toughness to be able to withstand the frustrations and disappointments that can be involved in handling an im-

portant project on your own. If a subordinate has not yet built this kind of inner strength, he may not be ready for delegation of important tasks.

2. *Discuss delegation with him*—without making *a specific assignment at that time.* Talk to your chosen delegatee. Make it clear that you do not have a specific task to delegate at that moment. Rather, you are looking toward a method of operation in the future. Under these circumstances he can, and will, reveal to you a great many things concerning his state of mind about delegation, without feeling that he has to say yes or no at that moment to a specific proposition.

3. If previous consideration and conversation satisfy you, *make a provisional delegation.* Provisional delegation works this way. . . . You lay out for the subordinate everything he needs to know and give him all of the tools and authority necessary. *But,* you say, "I'll be working with you for the first stage of this project." And you do work with him; you do not send him right off on his own. At the same time, he understands that you are going to phase yourself out of the operation. He has you around so he can ask questions without feeling that he is not handling his responsibility, and you can observe closely the speed and facility with which he moves into the assignment.

4. *Phase yourself out—with built-in check points.* Pull out of the operation, and let him handle it on his own. However, before you pull out altogether, set up specific and formal "points" at which the operation will be reviewed. Talk about this as a normal part of the delegation procedure. Now the subordinate is operating on his own, but he knows that he will have an opportunity to discuss things with you. He may not take the initiative to come in to ask questions.

5. *Continue to review the delegatee unobstrusively.* If things are going well, you can space out your built-in "check points" to a greater and greater extent. Substitute for them a more informal, occasional drop-in chat. During such a visit, the delegated subordinate has a chance to raise questions; but he doesn't have to. Meanwhile, keep yourself informed of his performance. If he

seems to be getting into trouble, go out of your way to make yourself available for advice.

Here's how the method might work out in practice.

Department head Steve Fine is looking for a delegatee. There are two possibilities. Bill Toomey is young, bright and innovative. Toomey is also quick on the trigger sometimes. Last week, he really let one of the production supervisors have it for not getting a modification installed on time.

Fine decides that, smart as Toomey is, he does not yet have the toughness and maturity to handle an important delegated job. So he picks his other possibility—Marty Corbett, a level-headed, experienced assistant.

Steve Fine calls Corbett in and says, "Marty, we don't know whether or not we're going to have to tool up for that special run, but if we do, I want to be ready. You must have been giving it some thought. What are your ideas on it?"

Corbett responds with some suggestions. They kick it around, and Fine is satisfied. A week later he talks with Corbett again and says, "Marty, I'm going to turn this job over to you *part way*. I'd like to keep my hand in, but you'll handle the lion's share of the work. You tell me specifically what you need in the way of people and equipment. You can give me that information this afternoon. And then, let's get together every day at five, for a review and a look ahead at the next day."

The operation progresses well, so one day Fine tells Corbett, "I don't think it's necessary for us to meet regularly every day. Let's set our next meeting for Wednesday. However, I'll be here every day at five, available if you want to talk anything over."

Fine continues to get daily reports on output. He manages to "run into" Corbett when there is something he wants to say. But, more and more, he pulls out and leaves the project to the subordinate.

This gradual approach to delegation is psychologically sound for both individuals. The subordinate does not have the panicky feeling of being thrown in "to sink or swim," and the manager knows that he is not letting things get out of his hands too fast.

THE RIGHT PSYCHOLOGICAL MOMENT
TO GIVE AN INSPIRATIONAL PUSH

We have discussed ways in which you can keep up motivational momentum in your operation. If you have:

. . . structured the operation to take individual workers' differences into account;
. . . handled assignments so as to win maximum initial enthusiasm;
. . . eliminated demotivators to the greatest degree possible;
. . . and delegated according to sound psychological principles. . . there is one more thing to bear in mind that will help in keeping up momentum.

This is the occasional "booster shot" or psychological push. Even the best motivated people can use a booster once in a while. Briefly, here are some of the kinds of boosters you can use as part of your managerial kit of tools.

Unexpected praise—commend a worker for unusual performance in an area he may not think you have been watching.
Additional incentive—offer a short-term reward, even a modest one such as a free lunch, for exceptional effort.
Evidence of company recognition—let people know that others outside the operation are watching and approving. For example, you can circulate and post a commendatory letter from the president.
Then there is the familiar "kick in the pants" method. With certain people there is no substitute for it. Handled simply, without laying too much stress on it, you just say, "Hey Jim— better get on the ball!"

Sports managers and coaches use every tool at their command to keep up momentum. And the maintenance of morale and momentum can make you a winning manager.

NEW PSYCHOLOGICAL INSIGHTS INTO STATUS-SEEKING THAT YOU CAN USE TO INCREASE PRODUCTIVITY

"I think *I'm* entitled to the corner office . . . "How come Lucy has a brand new typewriter when I have to get along with a two-year-old one"?. . . "If *he* is on that committee, I should be, too". . . "I don't think that somebody in my position should be asked to do that kind of work. . ."

And so it goes. The status-seeking propensities of subordinates can drive managers crazy. Furthermore, a lot of managers feel guilty about their *own* drive for status. We often hear the same type of lament, as voiced to us in this particular case by an executive vice president of a large service organization: "Why can't I find some people who will roll up their sleeves and go to work without worrying about where they stand in the pecking order?"

The reason that this vice president can't find such people is deeply rooted in human nature. Let's face it—no society or organization can function without differences in rank, authority or prestige. Our prehistoric ancestors sought status, just as we seek it today.

So the answer for the hard-pressed manager is not to *fight* the "status syndrome," *but to make it work for you.* Psychologists have been studying this basic human need, and their new findings now make it possible for you to use status as a very effective motivating tool.

Here is one of the best practical proofs of the prevalence of the status drive. Some companies go to great extremes to emphasize the distances between ranks of personnel. They provide special high level executive dining rooms, washrooms and transportation arrangements to reinforce in everyone's mind "who is who" in that company.

In other companies, a conscious effort is made to minimize status differences. Management boasts that "everyone is treated the same."

However, it has been found that in companies which play *down* distinctions, people create their own marks of status. Furthermore, those in the lower ranks *want* the status of their superiors to be recognized. After all, they aspire to reach the heights themselves someday. Of course, there is a negative side. Status can become an end in itself. Work is not done because of a feeling of craftsmanship. Non-work, or even disruptive activities, may be valued as a way of winning status approval. The unwillingness to perform tasks associated with lower ranking jobs can stand in the way of effective performance.

Certain companies tend to attract employees who are more sensitive to status arrangements. Companies themselves may be ranked in terms of their prestige. This prestige is real, since it often affects a man's ability to locate himself in a preferred position in the market place. It is precisely those higher ranking companies which attract the more status-hungry employees. You, as a manager, should know how your company stacks up in this respect. But regardless of the kind of company you are in, knowing about status *within* your company is vital.

HOW TO TAKE A "STATUS INVENTORY"

Look at the distribution of privileges, comforts and physical objects to employees. Note what distinguishes top management from middle management, supervisory and various levels of skilled labor.

Take the possession of an office, for example. Where is it located? What is its size? Does it have carpeting? If so, what kind of carpeting? Does it contain noninstitutional furniture? Does it have windows on several walls? All of these may be important clues to the status of the individual occupying that office.

People realize the status implications of what they are given, and they fight vigorously to acquire the visible symbols of superior position. True, money is important, but symbols are important, too. A worker can't go around showing people his paycheck to indicate that he got a raise; he needs some more indirect means of proof.

We tend to think of status symbols as being confined to the

middle and upper reaches of management. But the need for status is just as great at the lower levels. There are many ways in which you, as a manager, can confer status on rank-and-file people:

Letting preferred employees have first choice of equipment. A bakery firm gives its best route salesmen the newest delivery vans, and finds that drivers work harder to get and keep this privilege.

Giving employees options on setting their own priorities. The supervisor of a mail-order section calls in his prize producer and says, "You're good enough so that you don't have to stick to the plan of the day. You decide what you want to do first." The employee is pleased and motivated.

Offering prized locations. The head of the typing pool assigns the desk nearest the window with the best view to the typist who is most productive. Awards, plaques and certificates of merit. The boss of a key-punch operation sends his top performer a congratulatory memo in large type, which she displays at her work station.

"Luxury" furnishings. The consistently reliable records clerk is given an original painting to hang in her working compartment.

A status symbol is anything that visibly demonstrates that management recognizes the employee's value. This works from the top to the bottom of the organizational hierarchy.

One of the most interesting and economical means of conferring status is through the use of titles. This includes both descriptive job titles and titles explicitly signifying rank and seniority.

In a Mid-western insurance company, the turnover of file clerks had been fierce. Jim E., an enterprising department head, retitled the position, calling it *information control specialist*. The first information control specialist recruited for the job has been performing conscientiously at it for over three years, and gives every indication of staying on the job for a long time.

Think of a particular subordinate. How would he react to a title change? Will this change suggest a near-future salary raise, additional promotions or tenure? Will the receipt of the title so inflate the ego of the employee that his productivity will be diminished? To avoid grief, your expectations and those of the newly-titled employee should be discussed at the time his status is being revised.

There is a very close relation between power and status. Power is the ability or authority to control others. The drive toward "empire building" may seem pathological. However, the cause of the pathology may be the company itself, which rewards the "empire builder" with additional gifts of status.

Don't deplore your own status-seeking—it's important. Status determines, in large measure, the amount of power you have in the company. It also affects your chances of acquiring additional facilities and privileges which enhance and consolidate your corporate status.

Not only is your own status important, so is that of the people who report to you. Machiavelli wrote that a prince will be known by the kinds of people he surrounds himself with. The higher the titles, responsibility, compensation and qualification of your subordinates, the more status mileage you will acquire.

In planning your decisions, never forget their implications for your company's status arrangements. This dictum is expressed in the proverb "Vanity of vanities; all is vanity"—Old Testament, *Ecclesiastes* 1, 2.

THE IMPORTANCE OF THE "PECKING ORDER"

The idea of a *pecking order* grows out of experimental psychology. Although the original experiments were done with chickens, pecking orders have been found to apply to humans, and to the way humans behave in business firms. In the original psychological experiments, it was found that Chicken A would consistently peck, or strike with his beak, Chicken B, but that Chicken B would never peck Chicken A. Chicken B, would, in turn, peck Chicken C, which would never peck Chicken B, and so on down the line. Each chicken had a definite place in the pecking order, and his behavior consistently conformed to this arrangement.

Not only must you know your own company's pecking arrangement; you must also know the *reasons* for that arrangement if you are to be fully effective.

Human "pecking orders" have led to the establishment in companies of caste systems. A *caste* system is one in which the rank of an entire group is elevated and separate from that of another group. The chances of moving from a lower caste to a higher caste are negligible or nonexistent.

Caste systems can find their ways into business. For some companies, status differences exist between divisional and corporate personnel, even though their relative responsibilities may be approximately equal. Line and staff duties may also be the basis of a caste system.

The manager, being the people-handler, has to know his staff and what motivates them. Have you noticed that some of your people are more involved with the company status system than are others? These individuals can be your biggest assets or your worst problems. It all depends upon how sensitive you are to their special needs and points of view. The lure of future status gains may determine the amount of effort your people put into their jobs. The approval or awarding of seemingly small privileges for work well done may go a long way to maintain efficiency.

For example, what is the first thing the employee must do when arriving at work? This is important. The first few moments can set the tone of the whole day.

- Does the employee have to punch a time clock?
- Does he or she come through the plant gate or the office door?
- At what time does he or she arrive in relation to others?

Observe the mechanics of what people must do throughout the day, and the conditions under which they must do it. Sometimes even a small change can make a vast difference.

Workers under your supervision may be feeling a sense of

deprivation because workers in some other group seem to be faring better. A manager cannot be content to apply his own rules of fairness, or those which he learned in some previous organization. For example, if young people are rapidly promoted in a particular company, a manager must have good reason in cases where he bucks the system because he favors maturity.

Unhappy grumbling may adversely affect the performance of critical tasks at highly strategic times. Disaffection of workers may reflect poorly on your own leadership abilities, as news of this malaise spreads beyond your own department.

A highly skilled manager can maintain high job satisfaction and morale in his department, even when working conditions are far from perfect.

Recognition is the key. One manager arranged that the company house organ run a series of illustrated articles on "the men and women who really make our company go." These articles featured people doing jobs that were normally considered of low status. For example, a maintenance man explained what he had to know about cleaning solvents, how delicate machinery required special handling, etc. A similar procedure, concentrating on the specific know-how and interesting problems that come up on every job, was used to acquaint the personnel of the company at large with intriguing facts about tasks that had previously been taken for granted. Morale—and performance—went up significantly among most of those doing these jobs.

Dr. Robert Blauner, who has studied work satisfaction in various occupations, concludes:

> Jobs that have high prestige will tend to be valued for their status rewards even when objective aspects of the work are undesirable; similarly, low-status jobs will tend to be under-valued and disliked.

Your people will desert you psychologically, and even physically, if you are not attentive to their status needs. A status-frustrated employee may exhibit absenteeism as a symptom. He may also defect to some other department or to some other company.

A few such experiences make life more difficult for you and for your supervisors. Such embarrassments may be averted by planning for the distribution of prestige among your subordinates.

HOW TO TELL WHO NEEDS STATUS UP-GRADING

The most urgent cases for status-upping are those people who are highly marketable to other departments and companies, and who have not been in your department overly long. You may lose your best man if he thinks that moving will increase his status. Don't lose sight of status needs down the line. Chester Burger, author of *Survival in the Executive Jungle,* comments:

"Sometimes senior management becomes so preoccupied with its own status that it fails to pay proper attention to the staffs at lower levels. When management places an executive's name on his door while leaving the staff unmarked, it may indicate that they regard the rank and file as nameless automatons or menials, whose individual identity is unimportant because they can be replaced and interchanged like cans of tomato soup on a supermarket shelf."

Your concern with the status of subordinates should begin when they come in the door. A large food company hired a marketing man to manage their marketing intelligence system. Unfortunately, the space assigned was a cubicle. (The new man had been accustomed to plush offices in previous jobs.) His preoccupation with his meager surroundings was so great that it seriously interfered with his day-to-day performance. The uneven performance, in turn, led to management's doubts about the man's entitlement to the office he requested; the tension was resolved by his resignation.

Not everyone welcomes status with open arms. Some individuals have reservations about acquiring symbols of higher status. They may be concerned about the strain of additional responsibilities and the loss of comforts associated with their present situations. Status needs are no less important than talent as a basis for decisions about employee promotions.

What do you do about the employee whose thirst for status is seemingly unquenchable? Some considerations you will have to mull over: Are the employee's requests for recognition reasonably in line with his talent and his actual contributions? Does the company policy provide for such recognition? Is the company capable of fulfilling this employee's long-range expectations? Answers to these questions should determine the kind of effort you should make to provide for the employee's status needs.

Your own status is important for your morale, confidence, and recognition by others. Knowing what status consists of in your organization and where you are in the pecking order helps to keep you involved in a realistic way. Your application of the following principles will help you to achieve tenure, promotion and additional recognition in your company.

Work toward obtaining employee commitment for the company's status system. Emphasize its equities and benefits.

As a matter of record, not all companies are equally equitable. But you don't have to go out of your way to point out the shortcomings of your own company's system. You can go out of your way to make clear to your employees what your own standards are for someone to earn status.

Show your sensitivity to the status needs of your subordinates by attaining for all of them the symbols and privileges which are appropriate for their status levels.

Applying this principle calls for a resolution between how the reward system is applied outside of your department; what's available in the company; and the expectations and performances of your employees.

Do things for your people—even fight for them. But don't allocate status symbols all at once or over too short a period of time. If you do, you may be the victim of a subordinate attitude summarized by the following statement: "Yes, but what has he done for me lately?"

Merely obtaining status symbols for your employees is not enough. Try to obtain those things which the individual employee will value most highly. For one person, it may be the selectivity of having an expense account; for another it may be the direct contact with a key liaison person in another department, and for still another, rights to use the executive dining room.

Impress upon your people how much status they can command in the organization.

Status partly flows from the contribution which the individual makes toward the company's achievement of its goals. As such, everyone has status. As a manager, you can make abundantly clear just how the employee's efforts count in the total scheme of things. Equally important, you can bring home management's and your own appreciation of this contribution.

Your communications and actions with respect to those you manage should be directed so as not to deny or minimize their status claims.

Since most employees feel that their monetary compensation is somewhat less than is deserved, acknowledgement of their status claims is important to keep job satisfactions in balance. Denial or removal of a worker's prestige may cause him to focus on his salary as a symptom of his displeasure. Recognize the limitations of status in the reward system, and for good performers bring their compensations in line with their responsibilities.

One important criterion for selecting individuals for higher status supervisory responsibilities is their ability to manage and perform under greater levels of tension.

Dr. J. Diedrick Snoek reported in an article in the *American Journal of Sociology* that tension increases with responsibility.

This is particularly so in larger companies. In his study, Snoek employed a job-related tension index (J.R.T.). He obtained J.R.T.'s from a national sample of adults. Those surveyed listed which out of 15 common problems they have had trouble with. He found that 75 percent of those directly supervising some people and indirectly supervising others have high tension scores. This compares unfavorably with 36 percent of those without any supervisory responsibility. Before promoting someone to greater supervisory responsibilities, be sure he can take the heat off, because if it gets too hot, he may have to get out of the kitchen— under embarrassing circumstances.

Provide and plan for an improvement of "within-company" status for individuals as their outside-company status improves.

You can clarify the kinds of things you are willing to do to obtain rewards for those who perform.

Even if the company's reward system leaves much to be desired, your own maneuvering can make it seem equitable to those in your charge. However, you should point out the broad limits within which you can act. Otherwise, employees may think you are withholding rewards which are available. One useful technique is to periodically remind employees of the full range of rewards available to them in the company. People tend to minimize the status of their own situations, and this frame of mind should be counteracted.

An employee may have a number of years "banked" toward the nesting of his profit sharing. He may not understand the full value of his compensation, as compared with his salary. He may not be aware of the potential for status acquisition which exists for him in the job. How many good men are lost to a company because they define their jobs as dead-end, while their supervisors have been grooming them for higher responsibilities?

As employees complete courses, and earn diplomas and degrees, their values outside the company increase. In fact, mere tenure at a job may materially raise a man's status in the business community. Don't take an employee's loyalty or performance for granted, especially if his options become more and more attractive outside of your department.

A PLAN FOR MOTIVATION BY STATUS

Recognize the prevalence of the status urge.

Make it work for you—don't fight it.

Measure the status needs of your subordinates; do your best to fill them, and make sure the subordinate knows you are doing your best to enhance his status.

Constructively build the status of yourself and your department.

By word action, keep reminding people that you recognize their status, and the accomplishments that have earned them the right to that status.

By doing these things, you can turn what is a headache for some managers into a motivating tool for you.

5

Understanding How People Act

You are at the mercy of the people who work for you. No matter how decisive, intelligent, and experienced you are, you cannot handle an executive responsibility on your own. Left to your own devices, you may be the world's best problem solver; but this alone is not enough to get you through. The manager's primary job, says Peter Drucker, is *getting things done through people.* And so your chances of moving ahead and your whole career rest upon the activities of others.

True, your subordinates report to you. Theoretically you have the power to reward or punish, to hire or fire them. But the reporting relationships built into the organizational chart are not enough. You are judged on results, and results are a function of the quality and quantity of productivity that you are able to evoke from other people. And if you are going to get the most out of the people who work for you, you must be able to predict what given individuals will do under given circumstances. This is what psychology is all about.

FINDING OUT WHAT PEOPLE ARE REALLY THINKING

Even when you seek subordinates out directly, they will often fail to tell you the things that are uppermost on their minds. That is, they will not do this in an obvious fashion. But they *will* communicate in a roundabout way. To find out what your people are really thinking, you must use a certain amount of subtlety. You must, in the words of Theodore Reik, "listen with the third ear."

For, without realizing it, subordinates will reveal indirectly many things which they feel would be too risky to come right out with. If, in dealing with one of your people, you can move the conversation into a "safe" area, and then listen carefully to what he is telling you, you can learn a great deal about the things that are of concern to him.

There are several ways in which you can shift a conversation with a subordinate on to neutral territory, and thus get him to open up a little more freely. One technique is to use yourself as an example. Say something like, "When I was a supervisor I found that one of my biggest problems was that management simply did not know the pressures under which I operated. I would have two people out sick and a third not show up for a day, and then I would get a rush job thrown at me. And it always seemed as if the bosses thought I was making excuses when I tried to explain the circumstances. Maybe that's just one of the headaches that are part of the supervisor's job. What do you think, Joe?" Put words in the subordinate's mouth. Judge the extent to which he picks them up and adopts them as his own opinions. But don't indicate that you take his comments to represent his own opinions. Listen to what he says and watch the way he nods his head or gives other visual signals indicating agreement or disagreement. Ostensibly, you are talking about generalities as they relate or used to relate to your own experience. Actually you are giving the subordinate a chance to air his own frustrations and problems in a "low threat" context.

Use a third party approach. Quote the feelings of some other individual, probably unnamed, in the company. Cite his opinions. . . . "A guy over in Accounts Payable was telling me that he thinks the trainees they get now are not at all well prepared. Every once in a while I hear something like that from one of the other departments. You get around, Mike; what are you hearing?" In telling you what he "hears," the subordinate will be selecting those things which he will emphasize. In that process of selection, he is conveying a message to you. Heed it.

Talk to the subordinate about somebody who reports to him. Bring up a particular individual by name: "We recently gave Paul Phillips a raise—as I remember it was $700. I believe that was not as much as he was asking for and, maybe, expecting. Do you have any feel for the way he thinks he is being paid and progressing in this organization?" If the subordinate picks up the cue, he is apt to express some opinions about pay scales in the company. In an indirect way, he may be giving you information about how he feels toward his own progress and compensation. Tune in on him.

There are other opening gambits you can use to conduct what is, in effect, an *indirect attitude survey*. Here "indirect" is the important word. When you shift the conversation on to neutral, and therefore "low risk" ground, you are permitting your employee to ventilate his thoughts and feelings. He can do this without actually undertaking a confrontation, which he might think would be highly dangerous for him.

There is another reason why you, as a manager, should set out to collect thoughts and feelings from subordinates in this indirect way. Obviously, not every worker thinks that he is going to be fired if he says what is on his mind. But there are many people who shy away from conflict; they just don't like to "rock the boat." They'll put up with a lot because they want to maintain amicable relationships with others, particularly the boss. Nevertheless, there may be things which are bothering them. Problems which, if unperceived by the manager, will result in diminished productivity. By seeking your people out and conducting an informal, indirect attitude survey, you can keep your finger on the pulse of your department and anticipate human problems, before they grow into major headaches.

WHY PEOPLE "BLOW HOT AND COLD"

When you set out to discover what your people have on their minds, one of the problems you encounter is that many individuals seem so changeable. A man will say one thing one day; a week later, he is saying something altogether different.

For example, consider manager, Walter O'Brien, who sits brooding about a subordinate, Max Jensen, who has just left his office. O'Brien has been telling Jensen that a long discussed plan will finally be put into operation. The subordinate's reaction has been minimal—nods and monosyllables. The manager thinks "when I talked to Max about this a month ago, he was all enthusiasm. Now he's just a gloomy Gus. Can I have been that wrong about him?"

Jensen talks to his wife about the boss . . . "You can't figure that guy out. One day he's all sweetness and light, and the next day he's jumping down your throat. Just can't depend on him."

Both men are disturbed by changes in feelings.

The manager suspects that his change in feelings toward the subordinate indicates a weakness in himself. The subordinate is angry and disappointed; his boss "blows hot and then cold." It happens all the time—in the family, among lovers and friends, and in business relationships. When we, or other people, depart from the "norm" of stability in emotion, it is considered a defect in character.

But is such emotional steadiness a "norm"? No; it is an unapproachable dream. And our failure to recognize this leads to a great many problems.

We idealize the concept of permanent feelings . . . "We will always be true to each other; I'll be your friend for life." Jimmy Walker, the debonair mayor of New York, wrote a song called "Will You Love Me in December As You Did in May?" (They didn't.) We hate to admit to ourselves, let alone others, that we can lose our feelings of love or good will toward others. Our children don't act under this inhibition ("Daddy, I hate you!"), but we write this off as an aberration of youth.

CHANGING EMOTIONS

But the fact is that *no* feeling is permanent. Our relationships with others are constantly changing, constantly being renewed. As Gordon Allport said, people are always in the "process of becoming." And human relationships would be smoother if we admitted this. But as Dr. G. Hugh Russell observes in a paper originating in the Institute of Human Behavior, we are "aghast and angered with this 'notion' of temporary feelings, for it is true that poems and songs extol the virtue and sublimity of *eternal* love, friendship and care. Of course, we *re-experience* love over and over again for our children, parents, spouses, and friends. We readily accept our changing appetites for food, pleasures or social events, but somehow expect of ourselves that we must *feel love* as an unvarying sentiment. We would be more realistic if we accepted ourselves *as we are* with differing and conflicting feelings occurring temporarily and intermittently."

When you were a kid you liked lollipops. You probably haven't had a lollipop for a long time. Let's face it, our liking for people changes too. We cannot retain permanently the feelings we once had for even our wives and children, let alone our business associates. Of course, there is a carryover; we don't wake up each morning with a complete new set of feelings. But we do "blow hot and cold" because we are human beings and this is part of our make-up.

And this is a *core truth* that the manager should not ignore. Understand that your feelings toward colleagues and subordinates will change. Expect it. You hired a young man six months ago; one of his most winning characteristics at that time was bold self-confidence. But tomorrow you may be annoyed at his "cockiness." There is nothing abnormal about this, nothing to be ashamed of. Write it off as your feeling of that moment, and call upon your reservoir of good will to carry you over it.

The most dangerous thing about our variations in feeling is that we have a tendency to confuse them with our *judgment*. This is a perilous pitfall for the manager. We cannot altogether separate emotions from intellectual processes, but we should recognize that they do become confused, and do our best to keep them separate. You may realize all at once that you can't stand a man with whom you were formerly cordial. But this does not mean that he is any less effective in his business functioning. Feelings change rather quickly, but ability and productivity do not change all that fast. Keep your emotions out of your evaluation of performance.

DEALING WITH CHANGING EMOTIONS

When you feel spontaneous irritation toward a superior, a colleague, or a subordinate, don't try to fight it by struggling to keep the emotional relationship on the same basis as before. It won't work. Change the relationship. Don't see the other party as frequently. When you do see him, keep things on a more businesslike level. Willy-nilly, your relationships are constantly undergoing re-establishment. When you are aware that this is going on, you can give some rational direction to the process of re-establishment.

Avoid action in the grip of emotion. For example, take the situation in which a respected subordinate, with whom you have had a long and cordial relationship, resigns to take another job. Try to avoid moving too fast to replace him. Give your feelings a chance to settle. In this situation, we have seen managers make extremely emotional decisions ("That's the man!") without adequate evaluation.

You are changeable; we all are. No feeling is permanent. The continual, constructive re-creation of relationships is a mark of maturity—and a necessity for effective management.

Don't take the feelings and opinions of those who report to you for granted. Even though a subordinate may have told you something a week ago, this does not mean he feels the same way now. Keep your finger on the pulse; conduct a *continuing* attitude audit. When you are dealing with something so changeable as human nature, up-to-date information is absolutely essential.

WHY MORE MONEY DOES NOT MEAN MORE PRODUCTIVITY

Money is a topic that is often on people's minds. Managers are naturally anxious about subordinates who do not feel that they are being paid enough. Elsewhere in this book, we cover certain techniques by which you can give a subordinate additional psychic compensation without paying him more money. However, not every worker feels underpaid. When one of your subordinates is getting enough money, or even more than enough, you might think that he, at least, is in a good frame of mind and will be a productive performer for some time to come.

You *might* think so; but you could be wrong. Take the typical case of a manager—we'll call him Bruce Lewis. For a period of two and one half months, Lewis has been talking salary to one of his key staff assistants, Len Dozier. Dozier had been asking for a $2,000 increase. Lewis had not wanted to go above $1,000. But there is a project coming up on which Dozier will be asked to play a very important part. Lewis does not want to take any chance of the assistant quitting before the project is brought to fruition, so he calls the assistant in and tells him that he is giving him the full $2,000.

As Dozier leaves his office, Lewis thinks, "He looked at me as if I were Santa Claus. I don't believe he ever expected to get the full amount. It's steep, but I can really count on him to put out during the next six months. It's worth it."

But, having given the subordinate more money than he thought he was going to get, is the manager really safe on counting on a maximum effort? There is an increasing amount of evidence that says *no*.

Most managers are payroll-conscious. It is certainly not unusual, these days, to feel that some of the people on the staff are being paid too much. Union pressures, the manpower shortage, the inflated starting salaries of college graduates in certain categories . . . all serve to fuel the compensation skyrocket.

You're probably concerned about payroll costs. Maybe right now you are worrying about one or more subordinates who feel that they are underpaid. But, chances are, you don't lose much sleep over the mental state of the man whom you are overpaying. After all, what does he have to complain about?

Some, as yet unpublished, findings tell us this: *sometimes, when people feel that they are overpaid, the result will be lower productivity.*

One psychologist studied workers whose rates were jacked up to a point where even the workers felt they were too high. He noted an interesting phenomenon: as the piece rate soared, the workers became increasingly quality-conscious—beyond normal expectation. As this "quality-consciousness" increased, production dropped off.

Of course, as Dr. Edward E. Lawler III has observed, there are other facts that may cause a pieceworker to produce less than he is capable of: the man doesn't want to become a "rate buster" and single himself out for a critical appraisal by his employer . . . or he does not want to earn the enmity of his peers by "showing them up." Nevertheless, discounting these factors, the phenomenon persists.

Drs. Lawler and Ian Wood have been conducting some interesting research on this subject. We will not go into detail about the methods of their study, except that we are satisfied that they are able to determine which subjects feel equitably paid and which feel overpaid.

We have been fortunate to see the findings of Drs. Wood and Lawler. A key conclusion: "The results show that the overpaid subjects were lower producers than the equitably paid subjects. The results strongly suggest that piecework overpayment, *when induced by challenging a subject's qualifications, does lead to subjects being motivated to reduce their productivity.* Thus, the low productivity Adams reports for the piece rate overpayment subjects probably is not a simple 'side effect' of their striving for higher quality, *but represents a motivation on the part of these subjects to reduce their outcomes by keeping productivity low.*" The italics are ours, and these passages are worth looking at again.

How were the "overpaid" subjects made to feel that they were being overpaid? They were told so. . . "Well, since you've come all the way here I'll hire you regardless of this discrepancy . . . etc." How often does it happen in business that the manager, annoyed at the necessity to come across with a raise that he feels is unjustified, will express his pique by saying something like, "Frankly, I don't think you're worth it at this point; but I guess I'm going to have to give it to you." The manager thinks that the employee goes away feeling fine, thinking that he has "put

one over on the boss." True, the worker may well feel that he
has "put one over," but the findings show that he may not feel
good about it. He may, in fact, feel just the opposite, and his
productivity will suffer.

What may be happening is this. The worker feels he is not
worth the money he is being paid. This sets up what Dr. Leon
Festinger has called a "dissonance" in his mind. And the worker
resolves this dissonance by deliberately making himself less effective than he would be under an equity pay relationship.

So overpayment is by no means a guarantee of greater production. It may enhance the quality of work; it will probably
cut turnover, but it may actually *reduce* output. The increasing
weight of evidence seems to indicate that the worker produces
best when he feels he is getting a "fair shake"; no less and *no
more*.

Of course these studies have concerned pieceworkers. It would
not appear to be an easy matter to come up with any reliable
findings with subjects in any other kind of work.

Then might the same principles apply to people in different
jobs, and at higher levels? *The alert executive would be wise to
consider the possibility that they may.*

Nowadays, salary negotiations on the managerial level may
be little influenced by merit of performance. A man may demand
a large increase because he feels he has the company "over a
barrel"—not because he is so superb, but because the shortage
of managerial talent makes him difficult and expensive to replace
with *anybody*. Or, a veteran supervisor, previously satisfied with
his compensation, may be spurred to jack up his demands by
his resentment of the salaries paid to recent graduates.

You may have to meet such demands. But the research we
have been discussing implies very strongly that it would be a
mistake to indicate to the individual that you feel he is being
overpaid. He may feel that his performance has nothing to do
with salary; rather it depends on how good and how "gutsy" he
is in "conning" the management at raise time. Or, he may begin
to let his consciousness of overpayment eat into his productivity.

It seems best to maintain the facade of the strong connection between compensation and performance, *even when you are convinced* that it is being honored "more in the breach than in the observance."

HOW TO GIVE RAISES THAT REALLY PAY OFF

Every man has his price. Or at least that is the basis on which you operate when you initial requisitions for salary increases. When you hand out a raise, you hope you are meeting the price for loyalty, fulltime effort, and continued tenure on the job.

Nowadays, it seems to be hard to meet that price, or even figure out what it is. Management lays out money, building payroll costs to the point of near-strangulation. But people still do just enough work to get by. Or they leave to take another job.

For some managers caught in this inflationary spiral, the only answer seems to be to give it impetus by somehow finding more money for bigger raises, or to compensate by gimmick with deferred payment plans, bonuses, stock options, and all the rest.

But it doesn't have to be that way. A man's price for good work need not be measured altogether in dollars. Money may not be the only element in the equation. Indeed, right at this moment you may have at your command what it takes to satisfy a key worker, without spending a dime.

UNDERSTANDING WHAT MAKES PEOPLE WORK HARD

A few years ago, Dr. Frederick Herzberg of Western Reserve University stirred industrial psychologists with this technique of *job enrichment,* based upon his identification of *motivators* as distinguished from *"hygiene factors."*

Like most formulations that make a deep impact, Herzberg's theory is by no means universally accepted. It is rare to read an issue of certain psychological journals without coming upon an abstract that either supports or refutes his ideas.

Nevertheless, Herzberg has something to say to the manager.

One of our problems is that many managers have heard or read something about job enrichment or the motivator vs. hygiene theory, but they don't really know what Herzberg said.

Briefly, Herzberg maintains that income, *by itself,* is not a motivator for most people.

He says that there are two sets of conditions that affect the way a worker does his job. He calls one set *motivators,* the other set *hygiene factors.*

Hygiene factors can not satisfy. Their presence is necessary only to keep a man from being dissatisfied.

Here are Herzberg's hygiene factors:

1. Company policy and administration
2. Supervision
3. Salary
4. Interpersonal relations
5. Working conditions
6. Job security
7. Fringes

Motivators do satisfy. The most important ones are:

1. The work itself
2. Achievement
3. Recognition of achievement
4. Responsibility
5. Advancement
6. Growth

What's the difference? Herzberg puts it this way: the *motivators* "all seem to describe man's *relationship to what he does:* his job content, achievement on a task, recognition for task achievement, the nature of the task, responsibility for a task and professional advancement or growth in task capacity."

The hygiene factors "describe his relationship to the *context or environment in which he does his job.* One cluster of factors relates to what the person does, and the other to the situation in which he does it."

As we mentioned, psychologists are still debating Herzberg's theory. But the businessman does not have to wait until the ultimate validation of psychological findings (he would be an old man, indeed, if he did!) to benefit from practical applications of the idea.

The next time you are wondering how much you will have to boost John Smith's salary, take five minutes to ask yourself: "What would I do for Smith if I had no way to increase his compensation at all?"

Then apply these questions to Smith's situation:

Could I give him more responsibility?
Can his job be made more demanding?
What goals can be set up for him to shoot at?
How can I best recognize his efforts?
Where is he going? How close is he to getting there?

Give him more responsibility? Make his job more demanding? Here is where many managers are inclined to throw up their hands and exclaim, "It's crazy! Suicide." But it's not. There is considerable evidence, much too voluminous to cite here, that such moves do work.

HOW TO CUT EMPLOYEE TURNOVER

Dr. Joel Lefkowitz of BFS Psychological Associates specializes in the building of programs to cut turnover and make employees more effective. He states: "Objective measures of productivity, absenteeism and tenure have shown distinct and positive improvement in instances where increased responsibility is conferred." In his monograph *How to Diagnose and Control Personnel Turnover,* Dr. Lefkowitz gives, as one example, the stockholder relations department of a large utility.

Girls read incoming letters from stockholders. Then, depending upon the category into which the letter fell, a girl would pull out a model form letter and type a reply. The level of production was unsatisfactory, and the girls didn't stay in the job very long.

The job was changed. The girls became specialists. A letter of a particular type would be referred to a certain girl, and she had the responsibility for composing a fresh reply. Production went *up* sharply, and turnover *decreased.*

An important caution must be underscored here—*the manager should not become too theoretical about increasing job satisfaction.* He must sidestep the temptation to get hung upon semantics, asking himself, "Is this a true motivator, or 'only' a hygiene factor?"

The fact is that, in dealing with some jobs (particularly lower-level ones), hygiene is the only assistance that can be supplied, but it will help to make a man less dissatisfied.

Start with the concrete problem. Think of steps that will ameliorate it. Then, and only then, judge whether these steps are "motivation" or "hygiene." Why do you want to know it all? For one thing, the application of a hygiene factor gives only temporary relief, and you'll want to know that.

We were retained by an organization that does business through route drivers. Now, the job of the route driver does not come anywhere near being a plum. The driver has no status; he receives little in the way of training; he confronts frustrations and complaints at every turn.

We offered some medium and long-range recommendations for strengthening the role of the route driver (and his supervisor). But, there was one *immediate* step that *was* feasible, and that made a great deal of difference.

This step was based on some findings growing out of the area of military mental hygiene. Psychologists have found that the incidence of serious neurosis ("shellshock," they used to call it) among combat soldiers is reduced if they are able to talk to somebody about what they've been through as soon as they come out of the line.

Thus, front-line hospitals are staffed with medics who have some psychological training. They talk, or rather listen, to the soldier immediately after he has been in combat. And it has proved to be effective. To officers it means that combat troops can be returned to the line faster. To us it means that potentially serious psychic problems are handled before they become really serious. The longer the delay (in "talking to someone") the worse the problem becomes.

When the routeman checks back into his depot at the end of of the day, he is often seething with irritation and sunk in depression. He has a lot on his chest. At the recommendation of BFS psychologists, the company assigned somebody to *greet him —and listen to him*.

Just that. Now the routeman had a listener to tell his troubles to—a reasonably sympathetic ear. His check-in now is more than getting out of the van and turning over the receipts. He is offered a chance to go through a kind of *decompression experience*. He goes home a calmer man. And a man who is more content in his job.

It doesn't always take a salary increase to do it.

A FOUR STEP PLAN FOR GETTING
THE MOST FROM YOUR PAYROLL DOLLAR

Raises and bonuses remain a staple of reward and motivation. Here, too, management's approach often leaves a lot to be desired. All too frequently, compensation is awarded automatically, in unvarying amounts, without forethought or regard for the effect on employee motivation and morale.

It doesn't have to happen that way. You can get much more mileage out of your raise and bonus expenditures with the following steps:

1. *Hold a counseling interview.* Don't just pass out slips of paper to each individual, or stuff the pay envelope with a notice of salary increase. Make sure each employee knows *why* he's getting the raise or bonus. A moderate amount of verbal praise and personal recognition is definitely in order—and when the word comes down from on high, the higher the better.

2. *Specify a JND amount.* In psychology, there's a concept known as the Just Noticeable Difference—meaning just enough to be perceived. The salary increase should be of sufficient

amount to make a difference in the take-home pay, but not so much that you're considered generous with the company's money. Example: A salary increase of $10 might be a JND for an employee earning $100 a week. For someone earning $250 a week, however, $10 more or less is meaningless. Better make it $20 or $25, and give it the JND. Some executives find it helpful to set up percentage guidelines for use in granting raises and bonuses at various salary levels.

3. *Give it early.* Try to beat the employee to the punch. Anticipate his expectations, especially if you can't or don't want to give the JND raise. If he's expecting $25 more a week and you only intend to give him $15, he won't object so much if you give it to him six weeks early.

4. *Don't set a pattern.* Unscheduled but frequent small raises and bonuses tend to motivate men more than scheduled, infrequent, large raises and bonuses. Wait for opportune moments to reward an individual for a job well done. Example: You budget a $500 annual increase for a staff assistant. Instead of giving him the whole bundle as of January 1st, give him $200 in January and the remainder in $100 increments as he completes various high-priority projects (assuming you are pleased with his work). It will mean a little more paper work for you, but it will mean a lot more satisfaction for him. Here is a case where "salary," a *hygiene factor,* is actually communicated as "recognition of achievement," a *motivator.*

You must get more out of your raises and offer people compensation that goes *beyond* money.

WHY JOB SATISFACTION DOES NOT NECESSARILY MEAN HIGH PRODUCTIVITY

We have talked about how wrong a manager may be when he thinks an extremely generous compensation will always lead employees to do a better job. Another mistake that managers make is to equate extreme job satisfaction with high productivity.

Let's say a manager has been conscientious about conducting indirect, informal attitude audits with his people. He has one worker, in particular, who just seems "married" to the job. The worker seems always happy, never has a complaint. He is utterly satisfied.

But the manager should *not* necessarily be satisfied. Here is the reason why.

In talk and in action, we sometimes assume that job involvement, job satisfaction, and high self-motivation all amount to about the same thing. The man who is absorbed in his task must be deriving satisfaction from that task, and the individual who is satisfied with his work is motivated to do the best job he can.

Actually these factors are quite distinct, and a reminder of the distinctions is of more than academic importance to the manager whose responsibility it is to achieve goals through the leadership and motivation of people.

Here is a pertinent passage from some recent research conducted by Drs. E. E. Lawler III and Douglas H. Hall reported in the *Journal of Applied Psychology:* "The data seem to support the view that in research on job attitudes it is important to distinguish between satisfaction, involvement and intrinsic-motivation attitudes. . . Job involvement . . . can perhaps best be thought of as *the degree to which a person's total work situation is an important part of his life.* The job-involved person is one who is affected very much personally by his whole job situation, presumably because he perceives his job as an important part of his self-concept, and perhaps as a place to satisfy his important needs (e.g. his need for self-esteem). The amount of . . . *satisfaction* a person experiences on his job, on the other hand, depends on the *degree to which his job actually provides the autonomy and growth experiences he feels it should.*

"Intrinsic motivation is a function of the degree to which a person feels the satisfaction of his higher order needs *is dependent on his job performance.* In brief, job involvement may be thought of as the degree to which the job situation is central to the person and his identity. Intrinsic motivation can be thought of as the degree to which *attaining higher order need satisfaction depends upon performance, and satisfaction as the degree to which the needs are actually satisfied.*"

Jobs which allow the individual greater control and a chance to be creative are more *satisfying* then jobs that are low in these characteristics. But *involvement* seems to be as much a product of *individual* characteristics as it is of job characteristics. In other words, an individual may become deeply involved in a job that gives him practically *no* chance for control and creative functioning, or a job that is *not satisfying*. This individual sees his job as absorbing and important because of social relationships, personal security, etc.

We feel that this research points to the fact that *it is a mistake to suppose that, because an individual seems totally absorbed in his job, he is motivated to do it well.* And it is also *misleading to assume that an individual who derives great satisfaction from his job is necessarily driven by the desire to do it better.*

For an example of the first proposition, let's look at a somewhat familiar prototype: the woman who is "married" to her job. She has been in, say, the bookkeeping department for 25 years. She is first to arrive in the morning, and last to leave at night. She burns with loyalty to the organization. Obviously, she is *involved* in her job. But at the same time she may be seething with frustrations, snapping at people all the time, and finding fault with everything. The job is not *satisfying* her. Nor is she *motivated* to improve; just make a suggestion to her and watch the reaction.

Now for the second proposition—another familiar type, the manipulative salesman. He loves to "con" the customer over a lavish expense account lunch. He thrives on the battle of wits over the sale. He particularly exults when, through some stratagem, he persuades a prospect to buy even though logic would dictate that the prospect should say "no." This salesman gets a lot of job satisfaction, but he may manifest little or no *innate motivation to improve*. His job provides him with the autonomy to do what he wants, but his satisfaction comes from the way he uses that autonomy—not from objective performance.

It is well to bear these distinctions in mind, and not (as many managers do) assume that the person who is deeply absorbed in the job, or the person who is highly satisfied with the job, needs no additional motivation.

Involvement can exist even when the job being done is poor.

Satisfaction can exist without any concomitant drive toward better performance.

Intrinsic motivation is a function of the degree to which a person feels the *satisfaction* of his higher order needs *is dependent on his job performance.*

Take the time, now, to jot down the names of your "most involved" and "most satisfied" employees. Are you getting the best job you can out of them, or are you unconsciously ignoring them in favor of more obvious personnel problems?

HOW TO GET YOUR PEOPLE
OUT OF THE "WORK STATION" ATTITUDE

How many of your people have "retired" on the job? The organization chart tells you how many workers are holding down jobs and drawing a salary. It does not tell you how many are working.

Dr. Mark Silber, Associate Professor at Loyola University of Chicago and a distinguished management psychologist, has concerned himself for some time with what he calls the "costly incidence of on-the-job retirement." Dr. Silber asks, "What about those motivation-constricted individuals who stay on the company's payroll and whose corporate cradle-to-grave existence is not constituted of contribution, but rather, of performance stagnation?"

Executives are well aware of the problem of the "work-station mentality" that causes worthwhile projects to proceed at a snail's pace, and that sends the conscientious manager home at night frustrated and depressed. Professional managers know that one of their principal tasks is to somehow motivate their people to turn a higher percentage of potential into actual performance.

But it is an awesome job. There are no cut-and-dried blue-prints to follow. So much depends upon the manager himself, the unmotivated worker, and the circumstances in which they come together. But Dr. Silber offers some insights that may be of real value. He uses the term, *"motivation release from within."* This concept embodies two propositions: that motivation is not something that is *done* to a worker by his boss, but rather something that he does himself; and that the manager's most fruitful approach is to try to help remove the blocks to greater effort, and enable the worker to *release* the motivation that is bottled up inside him.

This approach starts with the understanding that no two employees are exactly alike. The manager must get to know each of his people, and this can only come through honest, open exchange of views. Dr. Silber cites Robert Louis Stevenson's observation that "the cruelest lies are often told in silence." He maintains, and we agree, that too many managers do themselves and their subordinates a great disservice by keeping quiet about unsatisfactory performance. We all know why this happens . . . the unwillingness to hurt people; the shying away from abrasive situations; the hopeless feeling that things are not going to improve anyway; and so a surface rapport may be mtaintained.

The manager who wants to be honest with people and help them to release their inner motivations should undertake a systematic process of observation, coaching and counseling. The counseling interview should not be confined to the annual talk about salary (and why, perhaps, the worker is not getting the raise he expected). In fact, this is frequently the worst time to do it.

As he gets to know his people, what is the manager looking for? In each case he is seeking an indication of what the individual expects out of his job. For some, it is nothing more than money. For others it may be companionship, or "something to do." Still others are looking for satisfaction, or pride of accomplishment.

Of course, most people are a mix of motivations. We tend to label them with the drive that seems dominant or most palpable, but as we look more closely, we often find others. The manager who talks with his workers, and really listens, may begin to hear that at least some of them do not feel right about their lack of contribution. These are the people whom Walter Lippman was talking about when he said, "Let a human being throw the energies of his soul into the making of something, and the instinct of workmanship will take care of his honesty."

How is the "instinct of workmansip" to be enhanced? By helping the worker to get more of a sense of *individual worth* on the job—and thus release the blocks to motivation.

Dr. Silber advises that the manager should cultivate the "three B's"—to *belong;* to *be;* and to *become*.

"To belong" . . . The worker's sense of belonging is enhanced if he knows that other people, and particularly his manager, know what he does and how important it is. There are many ways in which the manager can do this. One obvious one: when taking a visitor or new employee around, introduce each individual and say some meaningful things about that individual's contribution. Of course, to say these things the manager must know them.

"To be" . . . which means, to be somebody. When a manager knows something about how an employee was himself, he can work with the employee in a manner consistent with that vision. Many headaches can be avoided if the boss knows how the worker visualizes himself. Assignments can be tailored to conform better to the self-image. This is a lot easier and more productive than trying to change the individual to conform to the assignment.

"To become" . . . To fulfill one's potential. Each of us has two images: how we see ourselves now, and how we see ourselves *beyond* now. When the manager asks himself, about each subordinate, "What is he trying to *become?*"—he can see—not with 100 percent clarity, but a little better than before—*inside* the person.

And he can help the individual to effect the motivational release from within that can mean so much in heightened effectiveness and personal satisfaction.

6

Using the New Psychology in Your Relationship with Your Boss and Others

We've all run across the man who seems to have all the knowledge, intelligence, and decisiveness to do a superb management job, but who just "rubs people the wrong way." He can direct those he supervises, but can't handle those in the company who do not report directly to him. He can't get along with his superiors and his colleagues in other departments. So he doesn't move ahead. He attributes his failure to "politics." But it's not "politics." The fact is that a man who can't get along with his colleagues and superiors *is not a good manager*. He is not able to *get things done*.

Recent advances in the interpersonal sciences now make it possible for a manager to develop new and better methods of working with those in the company whom he does not supervise. We have examined the most pertinent of these developments, and have made an effort to translate them into plans and suggestions applicable to management.

HOW TO KNOW WHAT'S ON THE BOSS'S MIND

We often do not really *observe* others when they are talking to us. This failure to observe may not be of any great importance during a family conversation or at a cocktail party, but it *is* important to the manager whenever he talks to his boss. In order for you to carry on coherent communications and use the right tactics for persuasion, you must be able to find out what your superiors really have on their minds.

There is a way to "see" what they are thinking. Every move they make reveals their origins, their attitudes, the state of their psychological balance, and even their health. The expression on their faces and the comportment of their bodies can reveal their frame of mind far more than their cautiously chosen words.

Literally everyone speaks *body language*. Whether they are sitting down, walking or just leaning casually against a wall, they generate volumes of "classified information" about themselves. But this information is available only to those who can read it, and who will take the trouble to read it.

Understanding body language is not an abtruse art. If you pay some attention to it, it is indeed surprisingly simple. The reason that most people and most managers do not take greater advantage of body language is that they do not realize it exists.

Consider the situation in which you are sitting behind your desk talking to someone seated in the visitor's chair. The conversation is not a heated argument, but rather a muted and seemingly routine discussion. It is easy to assume that in such an exchange both parties remain physically immobile. Nothing could be farther from the truth. The next time you are involved in such an exchange, make it a point to look at—*really observe*—the other party. Not only is he not immobile—his body is *constantly in motion*. His eyes, his face, his head, his hands, his feet . . . one or several of these physical components are moving, and they are moving with an unconscious purpose. In effect, the body is a semaphore sending out messages originating in the innermost thoughts and emotions—messages which may directly contradict the words that are being spoken.

"BODY LANGUAGE" IN BUSINESS MEETINGS

The ideal forum for the alert body language "student" is the conference room. Let's go to a typical meeting. You get to the conference early and watch your colleagues filing in. There's

Tom Thatcher. He takes a chair at the head of the table, right next to where the boss will sit. You and the others look at Thatcher suspiciously. You are reacting just as you did in school when you saw a classmate pick out a desk close to the teacher.

Here comes Andy Hertz. Andy takes a chair as far from the boss's location as possible. He pulls the chair away from the table and cocks it back so that his shoulders are leaning against the wall. You can tell that Andy is getting ready to be his usual abrasive self, interjecting cynical remarks and breaking up the cohesiveness of the team.

Meanwhile the boss, Jeff Burns, has taken his place. Burns shuffles through some papers, then glances around swiftly, giving each participant a fleeting, impersonal smile. Everybody settles down, and Burns begins talking immediately. He talks for ten minutes without pausing. You get the feeling that Burns is emphasizing his controlling position. When Burns finishes, there is dead quiet. Nobody wants to be the first to follow the boss's act.

As the meeting goes on, Burns calls on various subordinates for their ideas. People tend to look at the boss or at their notes— not at each other. They are avoiding "eye locks" that might imply they are in collusion.

One man, Art Gingrich, seems to nod a lot while Burns is talking. Once or twice he says, "That's right, Jeff!" The meeting finally breaks up, and Art Gingrich's colleagues avoid him like the plague.

You have been present at an exhibition of "body language." Once you get used to observing it, you will become familiar with the particular body expressions of the people you work with— and what they mean.

HOW TO KNOW IF YOUR IDEA IS GETTING ACROSS

Imagine that you are in a conversation with your boss, attempting to sell him a new idea. You are fully launched on your presentation; he is listening. But what is he *thinking*? By observing him, you may be able to pick up some body language signals. Suppose, for example, he reaches for a piece of paper on his desk and pulls it in front of him. If it is a chart that you have brought in to support your argument, a reasonable inference might be that he is following you fairly closely and maintaining his interest. But suppose he begins signing his name on a pile of typed correspondence awaiting his signature. True, this is something a person may do, and *still* be listening. But it is more likely to be a signal that you are losing his interest. You had better invite him to ask some questions, or shift to a fresh tack.

Watch your boss as he listens to you. What is the configuration of his body? Is he leaning forward or leaning back? Are his eyes fixed upon you, or does he swivel around to stare out the window? What about his hands . . . are they fairly still—or is he "playing" with objects before him?

Stated this way, these things may seem to be fairly obvious clues. They are, but the trouble is that too often we do not bother to observe them. We are too wrapped up in what we are thinking and saying.

While the telltale gestures of body language will vary with the individual, there are certain ones which psychologists have identified as being fairly standard. For example, imagine you are in a head-to-head conversation with a colleague. You are negotiating some interdepartmental question. You don't want to "high-pressure" the individual, or push him too hard. But how can you tell if you are doing this? He is neither likely to tell you in so many words, nor is he apt to shriek in pain at the pressure.

You are watching the other individual. He has been sitting with his hands on the desk. Now one hand comes up absently and he begins to gently massage his cheek with his palm. A minute later the hand moves around and he is massaging the back of his neck.

Now these are unconscious actions. But they can convey far more truth about the situation than the words that are being spoken. Psychologists have designated these two gestures as "defensive reactions," stemming from childhood. They signal a feeling of being threatened.

There are other such reactions. As we said, they will vary in degree and style with the individual. Body language is an important component of interpersonal dealing. To know something about body language is to have mastered one more technique in understanding people by detecting clues to what they are thinking at a given moment.

To develop your aptitude at body language:

1. *Sharpen your observation about the body language of others.* Watch them while they are talking or listening, in meetings or in head-to-head conversations. Begin to spot the characteristic signals that convey thought and emotion.

2. *Develop a personalized dictionary of body language signals for the important people with whom you deal.* This "dictionary" need neither be written down nor be scientifically accurate. As you observe body language signals, you will begin to build a reasonably reliable "feel" for what really lies behind the words that others are saying.

3. *Develop your skills in reacting to body language signals.* Look for the gestures that indicate defensiveness, interest, hostility, puzzlement. Shape your approach according to the messages that these unconscious signals are conveying to you.

Every manager should be bi-lingual. Understand English and understand body language. To know what others are really thinking can be a great advantage, and with a little observation and thought, this advantage can be yours.

THE ART OF GETTING WHAT YOU WANT AND KEEPING THE OTHER PARTY HAPPY

You are often in competition with your managerial colleagues within the organization. (We are not talking about the struggle for advancement. We are talking about the situations in which you vie with other executives for good people, choice resources, scarce material, better equipment, more space, etc.) Some managers seem always to lose out on these confrontations. They are not aggressive enough, they do not prepare their cases well enough, or they ask for too much or too little. There is another kind of manager who always seems to *win*. He gets the best people from personnel, the biggest offices, the newest equipment, etc. But this kind of manager may be winning Pyrrhic victories; he wins a series of battles but he ultimately loses the war. This happens because in his victories, he so antagonizes others that he forfeits all chance of cooperation within the company.

As a manager, it's your job to get what you want and need to run your operation effectively. At the same time, you must get it without disemboweling your colleagues, and turning them into deadly enemies. There is a way that this can be done.

The noted New York attorney, Gerard Nirenberg, is pioneering the concept of "no-win negotiation." His premise is that negotiation between parties is only truly successful when at the end there is neither a clear winner, nor a clear loser . . . when in fact each party comes away from the bargaining table feeling that he has won something, if not all. Here are some of the principles of the new concept of no-win negotiation, as they apply to the task of a manager who wants to get what he needs, and not make enemies.

1. *Before the negotiation figure out your "must" list.* Determine your rock bottom requirements, or the top priority items that you feel you must have.

2. *Determine other items that will be "frosting on the cake."* This is a list of items that would be nice to have, but which will not cripple your operation by their absence.

3. *Document your case thoroughly before the negotiation.* Have facts and figures to support your case. Quantify everything that is quantifiable. *Visualize* your case by making copious use of easy-to-read charts and graphs.

4. *At first, go after the whole package.* Don't give up too quickly on any part of it, and don't indicate too early the items that are on your "must have" list.

5. *Employ the trade-off principle.* "Give away" some of the items on your optional list. Do this to win concurrence on your "must" items, and also to build up your line of credit with other departments. A point which is an option for you, may be a must for somebody else. Let him come away from the table possessing it.

6. *Use your reasonableness in negotiation to solidify depart-mental cooperation*. Let the other guy win some points. Later, when you need his cooperation, make sure, directly or indirectly, that he has not forgotten how cooperative you were.

By skillful "no-win negotiation" you can get what you need, and at the same time maintain relationships which are helpful and sometimes necessary to your success within the company.

HOW TO GET THROUGH
TO THE MAN WHO'S ALWAYS BUSY

No matter how skilled you are in understanding what others are thinking, or in getting what you want, your efforts will be futile if you simply cannot get through to the man with whom you simply must talk. Obviously, this is particularly true of the boss. One of the abiding complaints we hear from managers is that the man at the top is not accessible to them. It is frustrating and depressing to have good ideas and not be able to secure a hearing for them.

Recent full scale studies of top executives make it clear why so many of them are highly inaccessible. They work under heavy pressure and are subject to many stresses. The last thing they need is people who bring them more problems. So we find that a lot of top men, such as presidents, etc. tend to steer clear of interviews which may be headache producers. This is not always a conscious reaction; the man on top knows that he should be accessible and that part of his job is to listen to ideas. But unconsciously he may make himself inaccessible.

To get through to an "always busy" boss may require of you some tactical adroitness. Here are some principles, soundly based in the new psychology, that you can follow.

1. *Work with the boss's secretary*. Note that we do not say "*cultivate* the boss's secretary." Too many managers try to gain access to their superiors by "buddying up" to the secretary . . . kidding with her, giving her boxes of candy, etc. There is something patronizing and demeaning about this, and a good ex-

ecutive secretary does not necessarily have to be a confirmed "women's libber" to resent it. She is a professional; treat her as such. Assume that she understands her boss, works with him and knows what is going on. Don't make a full presentation of the idea to your boss's secretary, but don't insist upon altogether concealing it from her either. Discuss the situation with her frankly. Work with her to figure out the best way in which you and your boss can have a fruitful discussion.

2. *Prepare the ground in writing.* When a subordinate walks into an executive's office "cold turkey," the executive has no idea of what is about to take place. For all he knows, the thing may quickly degenerate into a "gripe session," and this is something he neither needs nor wants. Let him know briefly in writing what it is you want to talk about. *Emphasize the positive objective.*

3. *Surprise your boss by coming in with solutions, not problems.* Let's say you manage to gain an interview with a hard-to-see superior about a difficult situation. He may be fully expecting that you will come in and lay the problem on his desk. He will be resigned to it, but will not look forward to it with any enthusiasm. Provide him with a pleasant surprise by doing a lot of intensive work beforehand, and coming in not with a problem, but with a suggested solution or alternate solutions—not just off-the-cuff notions but well thought-out alternatives. Not only will this go particularly well, but you may be assuring yourself of an open door policy in the future.

4. *Don't make a speech—conduct a dialogue.* Some managers, long frustrated at being unable to get through to the man on top, "blow it" when they do get a hearing. They feel that they must get the whole load off their chests before the boss again shuts his mind. The result is a non-stop dose of oratory, which will at first irritate the boss, and finally numb him into a stupor. Relax. Ask questions, and invite questions and comments. . . "Do you feel that's practical?" Do everything you can to make it a relaxing give-and-take session.

5. *Get what you came in for, then get out and get moving.* Of course, you will have thought out your objective before the interview. Perhaps it involves getting the boss's acceptance of a

certain proposed course of action. Once you get it, don't overstay your welcome. Say thank you, leave, and begin to put the plan into operation.

6. *Confirm what has been agreed upon in writing.* Sometimes the boss will have the unpleasant experience of thinking he has agreed to one thing, only to find out later that the subordinate has interpreted the discussion altogether differently, and gone off on an entirely extraneous tack. This is not conducive to the maintenance of open communications. The next time around the superior will be highly reluctant to get involved in a discussion. So pin down your understanding of the conclusion of the meeting in writing, and get it to the boss right away. Make sure, perhaps through his secretary, that he has seen it, understands, and concurs.

By following well thought out, psychologically sound procedures, you can get through effectively to the man who is hard to see.

DEALING WITH A SUBORDINATE WHO'S AFTER YOUR JOB

As a general proposition, managers realize that any key subordinate who is worth his salt will be ambitious and striving to move upward. This is no doubt true of your subordinates. The logical corollary is that they want *your* job. Nevertheless, it comes as a shock to many managers when they find out that this is actually so.

It's not unnatural to be shocked when you discover that a trusted assistant would like to be sitting where you are. The question is what do you do about it. The worst thing you can do is fight it, or give any hint that you resent it.

Rather than resisting a subordinate's ambition, take advantage of it. Give him assignments that will test him to the utmost. This will not only enhance his productivity; it will develop him as a strong resource, and it may also help him to realize that there is more to your job than he may have thought.

For example, manager Luther Miles has to travel a lot. He must visit various branch offices to give a brief talk on upcoming plans and answer questions. Miles is not too happy with this requirement of the job; when he gets back to his desk, he finds mountains of work piled up. And then he doesn't like being away from home that much. Miles has an assistant, Lee Lauder, who is eager to visit some of the branches. He keeps trying to impress Miles with the fact that he knows all the ins and outs of the new plans and that, besides, he has been brushing up on his public speaking through Toastmaster's Club meetings. For a time, Miles has considered Lauder's eagerness a pain in the neck. But one day he thinks, "Why don't I try this young man on one of these assignments?" The manager finds that the assistant handles the chore well and is happy doing it. Meanwhile, Miles has more time to devote to the tasks he thinks are more important.

Look upon your subordinate's ambition in terms of your own. Face it; you want to move up too, and you have probably got your sights upon your *own* boss's job. By channeling the energies of an ambitious subordinate into productive areas, you are building your own chances. Ambition in others, as well as yourself, is natural—not unnatural, desirable—not undesirable, and positive—not negative. Admit that it exists, and use it to make yourself a more effective manager.

HOW TO MAKE YOURSELF MORE VALUABLE TO YOUR BOSS

Success in dealing with a superior involves winning his regard, his cooperation and his trust. What makes one individual trust another? Psychologists have not found the complete answer, and perhaps never will, but there are certain ground rules that you can use to build your "reliability factor" with the man above you. In doing this you are marking yourself a more effective manager—because you will be enlisting his confidence and support for the projects you wish to accomplish.

Here are five factors which we have found to be important in building a superior's trust of a subordinate.

1. *Be a source of good current information.* Industrial psychologists have noted that the higher a man goes in an organization, the more insulated he may become from what is going on. Partly this is a matter of choice; he does not want to involve himself in everything. Partly it is an inevitable result of the broad nature of his responsibility, and partly it is because people tend not to tell the top man what is going on. You can be a source of pertinent information to your boss, but make sure it is *information, not gossip.* And make sure it does not in any way reflect upon the performance of others. Sometimes, just a brief anecdote about something that occurred at a departmental meeting can give your boss a valuable feel for what is happening in an area that has become increasingly remote from him.

2. *Cover his area of least interest.* Your boss is not equally skilled at all facets of his responsibility—no man is. Nor is he equally interested in all facets of it. As you get to know him, you can come to a pretty accurate determination of certain areas that, while important, do not intrigue him. To the extent that you can *handle these areas for him,* he will welcome your help, come to rely more heavily upon your judgment, and recognize the fact that your efforts are increasing the overall effectiveness of the operation.

3. *Anticipate.* Routine subordinates wait for the boss to give them instructions or direction, and then react. This wastes time and places a great burden on the boss. As you come to know your boss and the operation, try to develop the ability to anticipate what the boss is going to want and need. At first make a few "dry runs"; anticipate and then see how well your anticipations work out in practice. Then, when you are able to, anticipate and move. When you conclude that the boss is going to want to move in a certain direction, begin to pull together materials that will assist him in his decisions. Prepare the ground for him. He will recognize it and appreciate it.

4. *Exercise tact.* There may be times when you have every reason to be justified in raising hell with a colleague. You may go ahead and do it, and a fair-minded superior will have to agree that you are right. But agreeing that you are right does not necessarily mean that he appreciates what you are doing. Use your

judgment in difficult situations. It may be best to hold back from "rocking the boat" for the simple reason that if you do, you will just be making a boss's already tough job immeasurably more complicated and difficult.

5. *Be willing to take on the dirty jobs.* Status is important to all of us. As a manager moves higher in the organization, he may well feel that he is no longer to involve himself in some of the more unpleasant tasks that were incumbent upon him at a lower level. And he is probably quite right in feeling this way. Nevertheless, "dirty jobs" do come up, and they have to be handled. The manager who is willing to step in and handle them, even when his status does not require it, is a manager who will be particularly valued by his boss.

Doing your own job well is an important part of your superior's trust in you, but it is not the whole thing. When you understand his responsibilities, and do or don't do certain things because of that understanding, you will enhance your value.

7

New Methods for Making the Right Decisions About People

The most important decisions that most managers make are about people. You hire people, you promote people, and sometimes you fire people. Every one of these decisions can have a profound effect on the way your operation runs, and on your own promotability to a better job. If you can improve your batting average on "people-decisions" by even a modest amount, you'll be a better manager. And you'll be a more relaxed one, too. For when a manager is constantly battling situations in which he is trying to figure out the puzzles presented by a diversity of human beings, his tension gauge is quivering near the breaking point.

In this chapter, we'll consider three contemporary developments that, when adapted to the everyday decisions you have to make about people, can make your performance a lot better and your life a lot easier.

THE PSYCHOLOGY OF INSTINCTIVE DECISION-MAKING

In this computerized age, we have grown wary of "seat-of-the-pants" decisions. Most managers are able to put together a mass of data that more or less bears upon all their choices, including particularly those affecting staff assignments.

Let's examine two simultaneous examples of "people-decisions" at Capulet Products.

Gene Fogel was faced with a problem when Ted Wellender, one of his key people, quit suddenly. Wellender had been a reliable and valuable section leader for several years. There were two prominent candidates for the spot. One, Jesse King, was an old-timer with Capulet—a plodding work-horse type, who had never come up with anything approaching a brilliant idea, but who had never fallen down on an assignment either. The other candidate was Alex Newmark. Newmark, a younger, more innovative man, had made some mistakes, but he showed a lot of promise.

Fogel's initial feeling was to promote Newmark. He liked Newmark better than King, responded to his ideas, and considered him a better bet for the future. But Gene Fogel drew back from making the decision purely on that kind of instinct. In fact, Fogel did more than draw back; he forced himself to be actively mistrustful of his own first impulse. Any decision that came that easily, he reasoned, was bound to be suspect.

So Fogel went to the other extreme and asked himself, "Why shouldn't I promote Jesse King?" The more information he collected, the less able he was to come up with answers to that question. On paper, King's credentials were, while not overwhelming, certainly highly respectable. So finally, after doing his best to view the situation with absolutely no bias, Fogel chose Jesse King for the job.

While this was going on, an important job opened up in another department at Capulet. Here the manager, Stan Polanski, had three choices for promotion. Right off the bat, Polanski found himself leaning toward one of the three—Jack Bowen. Polanski did not move right away. He summoned up the qualifications of the other two men and compared them with Bowen's. On the whole, Bowen came out ahead. So Polanski decided to "quit fooling around." He mused, "Why am I kidding myself? I want Bowen for the job." So Jack Bowen was promoted.

Bowen is working out just fine, and Polanski's star is rising at Capulet. But Gene Fogel is in trouble. Jesse King has not been able to handle the section leader assignment, and Alex Newmark, who was Fogel's initial preference, has quit and moved to another firm. Fogel wonders where he went wrong.

WHY YOU SHOULD HAVE
MORE RESPECT FOR HUNCHES

Fogel was not wrong in being reluctant to act immediately on his instinct. But he went too far in moving *against* his instinctive feeling. Stan Polanski, on the other hand, was more trusting of his first impulse. He checked it out, and then went with it.

And this brings us to an important point that sometimes seems to have become all but lost in the welter of scientific decision-making tools and mountains of data that surround us today. When faced with a decision, *your first instinct may very well be the best thing you can do*.

Researchers are probing deeply into this mysterious matter of instinct. Ethnologists study the habit patterns of lower animals, and come up with valuable insights into the behavior of human beings. As we study the results of current experimentation, we find growing evidence that instinctual reactions should be given greater weight than we are inclined to accord them.

Certainly it is well not to act impulsively. Get enough facts to check out your instinctive reaction. But don't forget it, or discard it out of hand. What we are learning is that instinct is not aberration. The "hunch" that says to you, "here's the man to promote," may be the result of an extremely complex process going on in your subconscious mind. We have a lot to learn about instinct; but it does appear that, faced with a challenge, the mind (in computer-like fashion) swiftly sums up the accrued product of years of experience and observation and suggests the best possible answer.

We are not aware of the process. We are aware only of the result—the "hunch" that pops up unbidden. And, of course, we know that not all hunches are fully worthy of trust. Thus, we too often throw out the baby with the bathwater. We are so suspicious of instinct that, in many cases, we deliberately take a course opposite to that indicated by the "hunch."

Don't do it. You can make the decision-process easier and more rational by giving serious consideration to your instinctive reaction to a situation. Write your hunch down. Flesh it out. Ask yourself tough questions about it. If there is no immediate and obviously crippling drawback that becomes apparent, go further. Collect information, but don't get carried away. Get facts that have a real bearing on the decision. And, if your initial feeling seems to check out, then you may well find that it is the best course for you to take. More and more scientific experimentation indicates that this is so. We are learning that our "hunches" are often mental "print-outs" based on years of input, weighed and calculated by the finest of all computers—the human brain.

A FIVE-STEP PROCEDURE
FOR USING SOUND INSTINCT IN PEOPLE-DECISIONS

1. *Record your first instinct.* When the problem comes up, write down the "what" and "why" of your initial feelings about it.

2. *Establish your first instinct as a working hypothesis.* Don't act instantly on your hunch, but set it up as a mark to shoot at.

3. *Play Devil's Advocate.* Attack your instinctive choice from every angle. Ask the toughest questions you can.

4. *Evaluate the alternatives.* At this point, look over the other possible course of action with the same tough objectivity you have applied to your first impulse.

5. *If your instinctive decision stands up, act on it.* Having subjected your working hypothesis to rigorous examination and testing, judge how it looks now. Still okay? Then go ahead. Chances are it's your best decision.

A NEW METHOD OF LEARNING
ABOUT THE TALENT ON YOUR STAFF

In the previous section, we discussed the growing scientific feeling that initial hunches should be trusted in making decisions about people. This is based on the proposition that the manager will have received the right amount and kind of input regarding his people.

How do you find out what your employees have on the ball? By observing and evaluating their work, obviously. But not every manager is able to do this as much as he would like. So here is a technique, developed by psychologists, that you can adapt to better gauge the promotable talent at your command. It is based on methods pioneered by American Telephone and Telegraph at its Assessment Centers.

SPOTTING POTENTIAL VIA
THE "LEADERLESS" GROUP DISCUSSION

Jot down the titles of the key people in your department that fall under your command. Now think of the people who handle these jobs particularly well—now or in the past, in your department or in others. Then think about the people who have *not* worked out in certain jobs. What have they been like? What has made them different from the successes?

Now put together some leaderless group discussions. It can be done more or less informally. Make it a practice to get together with your people occasionally to talk about matters of general or particular importance to the company or to the department. Do *not* take the lead yourself. Leave it wide open for others to bring up topics and to develop them. Encourage others to respond freely. In other words, conduct "bull sessions"—but bull sessions with a purpose and with a definite thrust.

Psychologists are finding that the leaderless group discussion, or "bull session," can be extremely helpful in permitting people to demonstrate their potential in certain ways. (Indeed, it has wider applications; you have been reading and hearing how psychiatrists and clinical psychologists use group interchange in their diagnosis and therapy.)

The important thing is that the manager stay out of the center of things. He must let the others in the group take their own course. If a natural leader seems to emerge, he should let this happen. If conflicts arise, permit them to run their course. But always *observe*. Note how each individual handles himself; how he responds when attacked; whether or not his ideas encompass a broad range of subjects; etc.

When you have a feeling of the qualities that make for success in a given job, you have taken the first step in assessing potential for that job.

This simple, informal technique will give you a lot better "feel" for the potential of your people than a whole battery of formal, psychological tests might do. It is easy to use, and every manager should get the benefits of it.

A 30-MINUTE SESSION THAT CAN TELL YOU EVERYTHING YOU NEED TO KNOW ABOUT A MAN

Group sessions are one way to find out about your people. But there is another, more pinpointed method that can give you every bit of information you need to know about each person who works for you, and that can do a great deal by way of motivating the worker to improve himself. This is the appraisal interview—the face-to-face confrontation in which you and your subordinate talk things over. This can be a powerful tool in the hands of the manager who uses it well, and who moves it along to a desired conclusion without letting it generate into a gripe session or an argument.

The Organizational Behavior Institute has developed new guidelines for conducting a good appraisal interview. If you follow them generally, making judicious adaptations for the circumstances, you will have added a most useful management technique to your repertoire.

A good appraisal takes management skill of a high order. It is the essence of management. All too often it can deteriorate into an exercise in which the manager "gets something off his chest"; or lets the employee "get something off his chest"; or in which there is a tactful effort to "leave him laughing"—thus negating any good work which has gone on before.

APPRAISING THE VALUE
OF YOUR RESOURCES—YOUR PEOPLE

Here are some general suggestions for better management by using an effective appraisal system that helps you evaluate your finest resource—the people who work for you.

1. KNOW YOURSELF

One of the big problems in appraisal is the phenomenon that psychologists call "projection." The appraiser projects his own feelings and problems by attributing them to the man he is appraising. We can't eliminate this very human tendency from ourselves, but we can guard against it. The manager should understand and identify his own wants and needs, his own approach to work, his own reaction to authority, and his own moods and habits. Then he will be able to look at other people openly, clearly and sympathetically.

2. SIZE UP THE MAN OBJECTIVELY

A Yiddish proverb has it that "Ten lands are sooner known than one man." That's true if we are talking about probing into the innermost secrets of others.

The manager who wants to help a subordinate doesn't have to go that far. He should know something about the man's needs and values. What makes him tick? Is he primarily interested in money? Is he concerned with what others think of him? Does a challenge turn him on? Is he stimulated by opportunity?

The effective manager identifies a man's strong points and concentrates on them. The system works to its fullest potential when a man is enabled to become the best person that his abilities permit him to be.

3. DO THE NECESSARY HOMEWORK

Collect all the data that will bear on the interview. This is the raw material for effective counseling. It permits the manager to talk about facts and trends, rather than impressions or personal traits. A fact-oriented interview is more comfortable for both parties. More importantly, it is much more likely to produce concrete results than a generalized conversation.

4. BE INVOLVED

All of the manager's attention should be focused on the man; and it should be apparent to the man that this is so. Undivided attention stresses the importance of the interview, and gives the subordinate the feeling that his boss is interested in him as an individual. All calls and visitors should be stopped. The manager continues to present a picture of total attention by his use of "body language"—no distracting movements, window-staring, rummaging through drawers for papers. Undivided attention is the most useful form of flattery.

5. HEAR WHAT HE IS REALLY SAYING

Too often we listen to others with only half an ear. The manager who acts as if he has "heard it all before" is not listening effectively.

The subordinate in an appraisal interview is apt to come in with a certain amount of anxiety, and perhaps even hostility. When the manager lets him talk, the man "ventilates," gets it off his chest, which makes him more receptive to constructive suggestion.

The manager should show he is really listening by responding appropriately. Agnes Repplier observed, "A man who listened because he has nothing to say can hardly be a source of inspiration. The only listening that counts is that of the talker who alternately absorbs and expresses ideas."

Besides giving the manager a better feel for the subordinate, listening has another advantage, often overlooked. The manager may learn things that will help him in his *own* job. The art of good listening is a tool that no manager can afford to be without.

6. GIVE HIM A FEELING OF ACCEPTANCE

An appraisal interview can be neither a love feast nor an unadulterated attack. The manager must let the subordinate know that his strengths are appreciated. At the same time, the manager conveys his awareness of the employee's shortcomings.

When the manager points out those areas in which the man has not been doing satisfactory work, the emphasis is on the specific points. The manager (if he has done his homework) cities facts and figures, without suggesting in any way that he thinks less of the man as a person.

When the discussion runs along these lines, the employee can see that his boss has not given up on him. He is more likely to admit his faults and to talk about ways of overcoming them.

7. CRITICIZE CONSTRUCTIVELY

Criticism is effective to the extent that . . .

    . . . it is based on fact;
    . . . it is expressed impersonally;
    . . . it is specific;
    . . . it is made for the purpose of helping.

"They have a right to censure that have a heart to help," said William Penn. Criticism should be made in the context of building, not tearing down. Instead of "you haven't got the right attitude," or "you should be more careful," it is best to concentrate on details left undone, or extra costs due to errors. This assures that the criticism is always related to the job.

Except for the rare exception (perhaps when off-the-job activities adversely affect the company), a man should be criticized only in areas where he fails to do the best he is capable of.

8. STAY AWAY FROM SENSITIVE PERSONAL AREAS

Sometimes a manager with the best intentions will venture into waters that are too deep for him. He will try to counsel a subordinate about problems which should be handled only by a qualified professional. A man's wife may be giving the man problems, but this is none of the boss's business. Encroachment into non-job-oriented criticism or discussion will not only be ineffective; it will undo all the good that has been done during the more constructive parts of the interview.

9. ESTABLISH WORKABLE GOALS

After a fact-oriented give-and-take in which the subordinate agrees to certain shortcomings, the next step is to set up objectives. The manager should be sure that the employee is really in agreement, not just saying whatever is necessary to get the interview over with. This means the boss can not take silence as acceptance. He has to work to bring all of the subordinate's objections into the light. Ideally, there will be a combination of long and short range goals. The employee needs a big overall objective to shoot at, but he also needs to be "reinforced," or given a feeling of step-by-step accomplishment as he goes along. So the manager will want to define sub-goals—milestones on the way to achievement of the larger objective.

10. LAY OUT A TIMETABLE

People want to know where they stand. Many efforts at performance review have foundered because the man leaves the interview not knowing where he stands, and not knowing exactly what is supposed to happen next.

The employee is probably willing to try to improve himself at this point, and anxious to get started. He'll welcome a deadline for completion of the first step.

8

Handling Managerial Crises with the New Psychology

There are managers working in companies today who are "set" for the rest of their careers. These individuals can be sure of high esteem and special consideration by the top brass, whatever the company's overall situation may be.

The reason? At a critical moment, *they were able to respond to a crisis*. They pulled the company out of a hole.

The world at large holds special admiration for the man who is *good in a pinch*. In every walk of life, we honor the individual who was able to keep his head when all the rest were losing theirs; who steps into the chaos of disaster and sizes up the situation; and who then leads the operation out of danger into safety and success. We admire the soldier, the sailor, and the athlete who comes through in the clutch. Bobby Thomson was a routine outfielder for the old New York Giants baseball team, but he will live in the annals of the sport as the hero who hit the ninth-inning homerun that defeated the Brooklyn Dodgers in the climactic playoff game of 1951.

The business hero may be somewhat less spectacular, but within the boundaries of his career and his circle, he is no less well-remembered. The authors recall a company within which we were conducting a consulting project a few years ago. Part of the project involved the evaluation of people in certain management jobs, and our attention soon focused on one particular man—call him Frank Dalton. Dalton was an amiable fellow in his middle forties. He held a key job in the marketing area, commanding considerable status and a good salary. But his performance in that job, while not exactly incompetent, was certainly lackluster.

So we went to the president of the firm to point out that the selling function might run more smoothly and profitably if a younger and more aggressive performer were put in Dalton's place. We did not suggest termination, except as a last resort; but surely some less sensitive spot could be found for this well-meaning but only modestly-gifted fellow.

The president said, "I don't think I can go along with that. We've thought about shifting Frank, but he doesn't do all that bad a job there. And it would break his heart to be moved out." We asked why this exceptional loyalty was being conferred on this manager. The president said, "Let me tell you about Frank Dalton. Seven years ago we had a sudden and very serious product failure, involving a special line that went to a small number of our biggest and most profitable customers. The entire organization was dumbfounded. We could see the imminent loss of a large proportion of our best business, and we feared that the whole company might go under. Everybody was in a panic. Don't ask me exactly how he did it, but Frank Dalton moved into that situation and took over. He kept his cool. He uncovered the most dangerous elements of the crisis, and he formulated and pushed through—on the spot—a plan that was able to save us. I agree that Frank has never looked that good since. But within that one horrendous week, he accomplished something that we will always be grateful for. And I can't forget that when we sit down to examine Frank's current performance."

In the end, it was possible to find a training job that Frank Dalton liked, and to which he was much better suited than his line function of that time. But we were struck by the high regard that Dalton had won for himself by, at one rough moment, handling a crisis and showing himself to be the man who could save the day by working calmly and effectively "under the gun."

An exceptional case—most managers must rely on their current ability, not a spectacular feat in the past, to insure that their careers move forward. But the case demonstrates the enormous degree to which a man can solidify himself by showing his capability of handling a crisis.

As the president said, no one could figure out exactly how Dalton had been able to manage the bad situation so successfully. Somehow, with a combination of guts, savvy and instinct, he rose to the occasion. Probably he would never be able to do it that way again.

Every manager faces crisis at some time or other. Under the pressure or critical and fast-moving events, he has a chance to score a resounding success, or to make the situation even worse. This should not be merely a matter of luck or instinct.

Crisis-management has come under intense study by experts in recent years. Behavioral scientists are just beginning to develop some important insights into this vital area of human competence. The studies will continue and broaden in scope, because the recurrence of crisis is one of the staples of present day life, in business as well as out.

In this chapter, we will consider some of the first findings of the new discipline of *crisis-management,* as they apply to the manager's ability to confront and overcome critical situations.

HOW TO SIZE UP THE CRISIS

The manager's first few moments of grappling with a crisis can be the most crucial. He must use them to evaluate the situation and answer certain vitally important questions.

The first question: *How bad is the crisis?*

Here is a case of two men confronting the initial stages of a potentially disastrous situation.

Manager Charley Lusk and Assistant Manager Elmer Raskob reached the assembly section of the plant floor at about the same moment, summoned from different areas of the office wing. As they got there, they saw instantly that the line was not moving. Workers stood around in little groups, talking and gesturing. Three agitated supervisors yelled and waved their arms at each other.

Assembly was busy on the final stages of a special and very important run. Four hundred units had to go out that day so that they could reach a big customer's staging area by the end of the week. There already had been delays, and now time seemed to be an overwhelming factor.

One of the supervisors filled the managers in. There had been a complete breakdown at the paint shop. Each of the small components being assembled in the run had to receive two coats of a special enamel. The power panel on the big paint shed had blown. "They're working on it," said the supervisor, "But I don't think they have a clue about what's wrong."

Lusk strode down to the paint shed. He grabbed the paint supervisor by the arm and demanded, "What the heck's wrong?" The supervisor answered, "Darned if I know." Lusk released him and rushed over to the chief electrician, who was elbow-deep in the innards of the mechanism. Hauling the electrician to the side, the manager jabbed his finger at the other's chest and insisted, "We can't afford a breakdown now. How long is it going to take you to get it working?" The electrician said he did not know; he was trying to find out. Lusk continued to ask loudly for answers.

Elmer Raskob took a different approach. At the outskirts of the melee around the paint shed, he overheard enough to fill him in on that aspect of the situation. Then he talked to a supervisor to find out how many units had been produced so far. He looked over the stages of completion of the rest of the run, checked on the location of the supply of blanks and materials that were being fed into the line, and then retired to a corner desk on the plant floor. Raskob figured busily with a pencil on a piece of paper. Once or twice a supervisor approached him with a question. Raskob made his answers terse. Occasionally he picked up the phone, dialed a number, and spoke rapidly. Finally, the red-faced, perspiring Lusk had left the paint shed, cursing in frustration. By this time, the works manager was at his side, getting a fill-in. Raskob left his temporary post and joined the two.

"What have you been doing over there, Elmer?" Lusk was irritated. "This thing is falling apart! We're in bad trouble!"

Raskob pointed to some of the notes he had jotted down. "I've been trying out some ways we could work this. I don't think the situation is a dead loss by any means."

Lusk stared at him: "I don't see how it could be any worse! We've got to get this stuff out. . ." The works manager interrupted, asking, "What do you have in mind, Elmer?"

Raskob spoke calmly. "There are 127 units finished. We . . ." Lusk interrupted again: "But that doesn't do us any good! We have to have the whole order there tomorrow, and to get them there they have to go out tonight. And if that gear is down for another hour. . ."

Raskob went on. "Yeah, we have to get the whole order there tomorrow. Let's suppose they can't get the painting machinery back in operation today at all. Okay. I was checking with the Farnsworth plant. You know we still have that old painting unit over there. Haven't used it since we installed this one, but it's still there and Joe Broaca went and turned it on, just to see if it works. It does. The components that haven't yet been painted could be done on that equipment."

Lusk looked at his assistant as if he had lost his mind. "Farnsworth is two hundred and fifty miles away! How are we going to paint them there?"

Raskob said, "We can ship them there by air freight. We could get them on a plane going out at six tonight. They can be finished at Farnsworth tonight; we can bring along our people to run the operation. And then tomorrow the whole shipment can go to the customer, again by air. It's going to cost us some money, but it beats missing the deadline."

Lusk was at first derisive, but the works manager was interested. Raskob explained the details of his plan. The decision was made to try it that way. It worked. As a sequel, it might be noted that, within a year, Elmer Raskob was managing the assembly operation.

Elmer Raskob had answered the *first question first: How bad is the crisis?* While Lusk was joining the panic and contributing nothing but unproductive yelling, Raskob looked over the situation calmly; put his finger on the critical factor; thought about the available alternatives; and came up with a plan that best met the needs of the moment.

There was one thing more that Raskob did. Often people who are confronted by a crisis fail to accept all of its implications. They shut reality out of their minds. They seem to hope that by frantic words and actions, they can make the bad situation "go away."

Lusk did this. He got mad and scared, and so shut himself off from the benefits that his experience and intelligence would provide for him.

Elmer Raskob, on the other hand, used effective *self-psychology*. He forced himself to face the worst, and then worked within that framework. True, the situation may not always be as bad as it first appears, but the manager who panics will never find that out. Only the manager who coolly assumes the worst, and then attempts to find answers, will discover the right answers.

A PLAN FOR MOVING INTO A CRISIS SITUATION

When you first meet a crisis situation, here are the ground rules to follow:

1. Avoid hasty and ill-advised action

. . . Don't start talking right away;

. . . Look and listen to size up the situation as best you can;

. . . While you may not be able to abate the initial panic into which others may have gotten themselves (and it may be a waste of time to try to do it right at that point), you can keep yourself free from joining the panic yourself.

2. Look for the critical factor in the crisis

. . . When disaster looms, it sometimes seems as if everything is coming apart at once. But there is usually one key element.

. . . Examine the dimensions of people, things, money and time. Focus on the one element that is primary in creating the crisis. (In this case the people were all right. Lusk mistakenly focused on a *thing*—the painting mechanism. But Raskob properly saw that the real dimension within which the crisis was taking place was *time*.)

3. Concentrate your initial thinking on the critical factor

. . . Subordinate all other considerations to the one dominant element;

. . . Frame your possible solutions first as to how they affect the critical factor; consider the others as secondary. (Raskob's solution involved spending some money, moving some people, using an older piece of equipment—but it went to the heart of the crisis—the *time* factor.)

4. Pick the best alternative

. . . Enumerate a few possible solutions;

. . . Don't get bogged down looking for "other" solutions— stick with those that come readily to mind;

. . . Pick the one that works best.

When you follow this simple checklist you can make the most efficient use of your brain during the first few critical moments, and you may come up with the answer right away.

HOW TO BE SURE YOU WON'T MAKE THINGS WORSE

Within the past few years, the medical profession has become increasingly concerned about a phenomenon called "iatrogenic intervention." This concerns the situations in which the treatment of a physician exacerbates the patient's complaint. To put it in more familiar terms, the doctor makes you sicker. One example is the case of the doctor who prescribes an antibiotic to clear up a superficial ailment, only to observe that the patient has a violent reaction to the drug resulting in a far more serious illness than the original.

The manager who is called on to interject himself into a crisis situation can sometimes make the situation a lot worse, if he isn't careful. This is particularly true in circumstances where the crisis stems from anger, alienation or depression affecting a sizeable number of his workers. Here's an example.

At Rockwell Savings and Trust Company, there are approxi-

mately 30 girls of mixed racial background reporting to Bob
Daley. The group breaks down to 67 percent white, 32 percent
black and approximately 1 percent oriental. The black and white
girls had been getting along very well, perhaps unusually well.
The girls had a monthly theatre party, they visited each other's
homes, and they frequently went out together with their husbands
or boy friends. Daley was quite proud of the situation.

However, he recently hired a new black girl, Joan Welden.
He grew concerned that her appearance and manner looked a
little too "militant and black national." He became even more
sensitive when a couple of the white girls started to talk about her
a little negatively.

Daley called Joan Welden into his office on the pretense of a
performance review. He talked about the congeniality or sense of
brotherhood in their work group, at no time expressing his true
concerns. He said that while there was no dress or appearance
code, it was "nice" that everybody seemed to more or less take
some care about these matters. Joan Welden left Daley's office
puzzled and annoyed. The other workers assumed that he had
"bawled her out"—without results. Within two to three weeks
there was almost complete polarization of the two groups, with a
real physical fight between two girls.

Daley went into a potentially dangerous situation, and made it
actually critical. By beating around the bush with Joan Welden,
and at the same time failing to take any steps to reduce the tension among the large number of disaffected employees, he sharpened the polarization to a super-crisis stage.

What should Bob Daley have done?

First, he should have avoided prejudgments. He should have
given himself more time to ascertain the true proportions of the
difficulty, and he should have given the situation more time to
clear itself up.

Then, he should have come to some logical conclusions. Was
it just the way Joan Welden *looked* that had turned the group
against her? If so, then there were two choices. Daley might try
to get Joan Welden to change her visual style; we would not
recommend that. Or, he might have taken steps to emphasize the

idea that how a person looks is not nearly as important as how he or she acts.

Once Daley had made his decision, he should have tried to diminish the crisis through positive reinforcement, rather than by vague threats or recriminations. He could have made it a point to be cordial to Joan Welden in front of the group, and he could have shown himself as appreciative of the efforts of others to accept the newcomer.

By taking a few simple measures, Daley would have made sure that he did not make the situation worse. He would have relaxed the tension gradually. And he would have permitted the positive factors within the department to work for him.

POSITIVE STEPS TO CONTROL GROUP CRISIS

1. *Consider each situation on its own merits rather than acting automatically.* It is important to distinguish between those situations that are truly unusual and need your immediate attention, as opposed to those that may appear unpleasant but are not critical. The fact that there is some dissension among some employees may reflect a personal difficulty, and not a widespread problem.

2. *Show concern when the occasion warrants, but respect each individual's right to be left alone.* "Concern is the key word. As a manager you must show concern, but give each person the opportunity to act. It must be assumed that if a person is working in the company, then he is capable of doing his particular job.

3. Keep in mind that *words speak louder than actions.* The nicest action in the world can be ruined by accompanying it with patronizing or ill-considered words.

4. Once you've diagnosed the problem, ask yourself (like every doctor does) *whether or not it will get better simply with the passage of time.* Bob Daley's problem may have "escalated" somewhat, but it is more likely that it would have settled down within a short time.

5. *Allow subordinates the maximum opportunity to solve their*

own problems and perhaps even learn from their mistakes. This is not to suggest that the employee should be allowed to make irreversible mistakes; however, he should be allowed some independence.

6. When it is actually necessary to change an employees' behavior, *use positive reinforcement rather than threats or recriminations.*

7. In discussing the work with your employees, *state* your position calmly and without emotion. Similarly, *don't try to be rational with a person who is emotionally upset.* Wait out the storm patiently.

8. *Don't expect your subordinates to react to situations exactly as you do.* As people work together, they have time to adapt to each other and learn from each other. This may come to pass without an active attempt to change one another.

9. No matter how harassed you may be, in the short run, *never underestimate the respect and authority that supervisors have in the uses of subordinates.* From the power of this relationship comes the basic iatrogenic principle that when you intervene in any situation involving subordinates, you immediately change its nature, and can make it worse as easily as you can make it better.

By keeping in mind the possible iatrogenic effects of your own actions, you will do much more than simply prevent harm. You will discover that the less you intervene unnecessarily, the more weight you will carry when you do intervene. Managers who do not intervene in all aspects of a subordinate's activities, but save the "heavy artillery" for the heavy problems, are much more likely to be successful when a truly important issue arises.

HOW TO SETTLE DISPUTES

Some of the worst crises that a manager must handle involve neither equipment breakdowns nor group disaffection; rather, they erupt as the result of disputes between two individuals. How do you settle a fight? Nowadays, police departments across the

United States are undergoing training to help officers mediate disputes. The authors of this book have participated in a number of such programs. The lessons learned in this new field of study can be readily applied to the manager's job.

You've seen the situation. Two employees get into a shouting match. If the matter isn't resolved satisfactorily, the work of an entire department can be disrupted. The residue of enmity can effect morale for months and even years to come. You're the boss; you're on the spot. How do you move in and restore order when a face-to-face crisis threatens the functioning of your staff?

First, *separate the disputants*. The worst thing you can do is to hear both sides simultaneously. Don't walk in and ask, "What's going on here?" The resulting babble of conflicting recriminations will drastically escalate the dispute. It is a good idea to bring somebody else along, such as your assistant, perhaps, so that the parties can more easily be drawn apart. Say, "Gene, you go into my office with Dan for a minute while I talk to John. Then I'd like to hear your side of it."

Resist the temptation to take sides. How often we hear the intervener saying to one of the adversaries, "George, you have to admit that Walter has a point there. You *do* tend to go off half-cocked when something like this happens." Result? A fresh outburst of volcanic proportions, leading to even further polarization, and the destruction of any value that you might have as an intervener.

Play it like the old Hasidic scholar in the legend. The husband comes in with his side of the argument and the scholar says, "You're right." Then the wife comes in with her story and the scholar once again says, "You're right." An onlooker to all this protests, "That's inconsistent; how could they *both* be right?" And the scholar turns affably to him and says, "You're right." Agree with everybody; don't let consistency interfere with your placatory role.

Don't try to "get things straightened out." You are not there to provide insights or make judgments, or to offer therapy. The limit of what you can acomplish is to "cool it" until the parties get themselves under some semblance of control. They may be breathing heavily; they may not be speaking to each other; but if they have temporarily ceased active hostilities, then you have done your job. Don't try to do more—you will regret it.

Refrain from ever mentioning the issue again. We have run into the situation in which the intervener does a reasonable job of cooling off the disputants, but then blows the whole thing a week later by asking one of the parties, "Have you and John got that all straightened out now?"

Nobody likes to be reminded of the time when he was out of control, and his reactions at being so reminded may stir the whole thing up afresh. Cultivate your powers of forgetfulness; act as if you had never seen these people, under stress, psychologically naked. Even if your offhand reminder does not bare the just-healing wounds once again, it may lose you some friends for life.

Overall, the keyword is *restraint*. Limit yourself to one task—the cooling down of hostilities. To attempt to go beyond that is to almost surely make the situation worse, and to give yourself headaches that will foul you up personally and professionally.

9

Using the New Psychology with Customers and Others Outside Your Organization

Your managerial contacts with people can be roughly divided into three categories.

You *direct* the activities of those who report to you. Your executive responsibility is to bring these subordinates to the maximum level of effectiveness and keep them there. Since you are the boss, you have a great deal of scope in telling them what to do and what not to do. And even when you are not issuing instructions or directions, your position as "the boss" gives you considerable leverage in dealing with those who report to you.

You *work with* colleagues in the organization and those to whom you report. With these individuals, you obviously do not have the leverage of command. But you are all members of the same organization, presumably working toward common and generally accepted goals. Moreover, you deal with these corporate associates within a framework of common knowledge of a "style" of doing business.

You *talk with* people outside the organization. These can be strictly working relationships, or you may be mixing congeniality with work. Your dealings with outside people can be quite useful, and sometimes they become extremely important because you are frequently trying to get something from these contacts—information, cooperation, actual business, or at least a favorable frame of mind.

Your contacts with outside people take place in a different framework from those inside the organization. You have (in the great majority of cases) no leverage. You do not have a common acceptance of ultimate goals or methods of conducting an exchange. You must be able to get what you want, but at the same time you must be cautious, because you are, at the given moment of contact, representing your organization. So you must be able to make quick and accurate judgments about what makes the other party tick, and you must be able to project a positive image.

And in most cases, you are trying to do this with people about whom you have far less knowledge about than those who work for you—or with you. So you need to make quick, sure judgments. There are developments in the realm of the *new psychology* that can help you to handle your outside contacts effectively and with a large measure of personal satisfaction.

HOW TO SIZE UP PEOPLE AS THEY ARE NOW

"What makes him tick?" When we have to deal with a man, this is one of the first questions we ask ourselves. If we can understand the basic motivations that make a person act the way he does, or the fundamental "drives" concealed beneath his exterior, then we can begin to figure out how to deal with him.

As we come to know people, at work or socially, we build up a feeling for what makes them tick. We form an impression of the things that they consider important, the circumstances that they react most sharply to and, on the other hand, the things that "they could not care less" about. For example, Ed Foster is an accounting supervisor who has always seemed extremely careful about details. He tends to double-check everything. He takes it to heart when even the most trivial error is traceable to him. So, to win Ed's maximum cooperation on a particular project, you might be inclined to say something like: "We want to be doubly sure that there are no slip-ups in this." And you would be likely to return to this theme from time to time.

But one day you might be in for a surprise. You emphasize the importance of watching out for small details, but this does not seem to turn Ed Foster on. He goes through the motions, letting mistakes slip through. And he is not too upset about it. Ed Foster's personality has not changed overnight. It just happens that, this particular day, Ed's dominant drive is *not* caution about details. Something has happened to him today; a combination of inside and outside circumstances has given him a different set of priorities. Your problem is neither to figure out exactly what caused this seeming change in attitude, nor to project how long it will last. You have to determine, quickly, what will best motivate Ed Foster right now to do what you want.

THE PITFALL OF THE STEREOTYPE

We tend to "type" people. We say that Smith is excitable; Jones is patient; Brown is "out for number one"; Green is a procrastinator; etc. And in a general sense, this "typing" may hold up over the majority of our dealings with the individual. *But not always*. At certain times, people "tick" in a different rhythm, even people we have come to know very well. So understanding an individual is not a "one-shot" process. We can't say, "This is what so-and-so is like"—and then base all further interaction on that judgment. We must keep looking at so-and-so, and continue to figure out what makes him tick *today*.

"Typing" people can be misleading and dangerous when we know them well. It is far more risky when we make facile assumptions about people whom we do *not* know well. And this is a big reason why so many "outside" contacts are mishandled.

For we all "type" people, even on first meeting, and on the flimsiest of grounds. You walk into the office of George Casey, whom you have never met before. Casey is robust and smiling, with an extra-firm handshake. He talks fluently, in booming tones. He reminds you of other people you have met who come on the same way. So your mind seeks for a niche into which to place the individual. An immediate process of instant classification begins. *And this can be extremely misleading.* In effect, your mind is doing something for which it is programmed. But you don't want to permit it to classify the other party that fast. You must make a deliberate effort to suspend judgment until there is enough data on which to make a currently accurate decision about what makes this person tick right now.

In most cases, when we meet people as part of the management job, we have some sort of advance inkling about them. We have heard comments. . . "This guy is a hard bargainer" . . . "You can't get a straight answer out of him" . . . "Money is the only thing that interests him" . . . etc. Don't ignore this kind of input, but don't let it influence your decisions about the other person too early in the game. Even if the preliminary information is accurate—and that is a big "if"—human beings do change. The individual you are contacting may tick quite differently today. And *today* is the time when you must get through to him with your message, and get from him whatever you are trying to get.

Your most important clues to what an individual is like today will come from what he says and how he acts right at the moment. And your most important instruments for picking up those clues are your eyes and ears. Does the other party seem anxious to get down to business, or does he seem to want to engage in small talk? If he seems to avoid the main topic, it may be because he anticipates that you are going to say something that he does not understand, or that you will pose a question that he is unwilling or not ready to answer.

With the hesitant individual, you'll want to go through the unimportant preliminaries. They may be just his way of feeling you out, or of permitting himself to decide that you are someone with whom he can talk frankly. And when you do guide the conversation around to where you want it, try to reassure him to the extent that you can. If there is something that you think may be bothering him, say something that is calculated to dispell his anxiety . . . "Of course, we don't expect any decision from you on this until you've had a chance to study it" . . . "I'd like to make it clear that we want to be fair about this; it's not our policy to hold people to commitments when outside circumstances alter the situation" . . . "Everything we say is, of course, in the strictest confidence."

Show by your listening attitude and by the questions you ask, that you are interested and involved in what the other party is saying. Do this because regardless of whatever mood he may be in, or whatever stimuli he may be most receptive to today, it will open up the interchange so that he will be more free in telling you what's on his mind.

Probe for further indications of what is on the other person's mind at this particular time. One good way to do this is through the "reflection technique" used by industrial and clinical psychologists alike. Essentially, this involves repetition of the other person's comments in a slightly altered and differently emphasized form. For example, if he has dwelt upon budgetary factors. . . "We budget for the whole year and try to keep con tingency appropriations to a minimum" . . . or you might say something like, "Yes, Mr. Johnson—I realize that, like a lot of organizations these days, yours may be under some more-than-usual financial pressure." He may wave aside the notion that there is any particular dollar squeeze that may affect the situation, or he may permit you to continue to entertain the notion. Either way, you will have a better idea of what is making him tick.

Another method of smoking out the dominant drives that impel a man's thinking at a particular time is the technique of the open end statement. You put forward a conjecture and let it trail off. You might say, for example, "There may well be some other people you'd want to clear this with before coming back to us with an answer. . ." He can take up the gambit and indicate that, yes, he is not the sole decision-maker in this case (even though his standing in the firm may have led you to assume otherwise), or he may assure you that he alone will call the shots.

HOW TO DETECT AN INDIVIDUAL'S DOMINANT DRIVES

These are a few of the most important approaches in detecting a man's current drives:

> . . . observe the eagerness (or lack of it) with which he gets around to serious subjects;
> . . . let him feel you out;
> . . . show your interest and involvement;
> . . . watch his physical reactions to various topics;
> . . . probe for clues as to what he is thinking.

By approaching outside contacts with an open mind, and by using your faculties to perceive clues as to what makes a man tick today, you will be laying the groundwork for more profitable and satisfying outside-the-company interchange.

HOW TO "COME ACROSS"
—WITH IMPACT AND EFFECTIVENESS

Making the "right impression"—this is a universal preoccupation among people who must carry on contacts outside the organization. In any confrontation, you make an impression. Whether that impression is favorable or unfavorable is a direct result of how you handle yourself within the span of a very few minutes.

Psychologists studying this matter of "impression" have determined, to some degree, the way in which our minds work when we react to others. Some insight into these new findings can help you project the image you want in dealing with people outside the company.

In the previous section, we cautioned against the tendency to "type" people—to make decisions about others on the basis of previous contacts or what we have read or heard. We pointed out that you will find out far more about what makes the other person "tick" if you approach him without preconceptions and use your eyes, ears and mind to find out what are his dominant concerns and drives at the actual moment of meeting.

This same tendency to "type" individuals, before obtaining sufficient evidence, *will work in your favor in making the impression you want* because the other party is subject to the same tendency toward prejudgment as you are. He is likely to "type" you before meeting you, or in the first few moments of conversation. There is no way that you can avoid that. But you can make an impact on him through *diverging* from type, in a manner that is most favorable to you.

For example: let's say that you have an appointment with another man to follow through on a certain phase of intercompany negotiation. The other man has "typed" you as an impatient, driving individual, who keeps the pressure on to come to a conclusion. He is on his guard—ready to be pushed and prepared to resist your pushing. That is the image of you that he brings to the confrontation.

USING SURPRISE FOR MAXIMUM IMPACT

But, a short way into the meeting, you *surprise* him. When an important point has come up and been discussed in a way that seems to cover all the points, he expects you to bustle on to the next point. Instead, you say: "We seem to have gone over every angle of that, but we want to make sure. So let's take a moment to think about it again. We want to make sure that all the questions are answered. You probably have some other point, even a minor one, that you'd like to bring up." You may even suggest a topic that has not been covered.

This will come as a surprise to him—a pleasant surprise. This is because you are not conforming to type. Instead of rushing the business along, you are slowing things down to make sure he has time to think about everything, and ask questions where he is not sure. This *departure from type* is the basis on which his dominant new impression of you will be formed.

Anything that surprises us substantially about the behavior

of others, or that departs from our expectations of how they are going to act, creates a new impression that floods out the pre-conceptions formed as a result of the human tendency to place people in convenient niches.

And this is the key to coming across with the impression you want to make.

Before meeting another individual, give a little thought to the prejudgments he is likely to make of you. If he has met you before, what were the circumstances? How is he likely to size you up now on the basis of the previous contact? If he has not met you before, what would be the logical expectations he might have about you—not just because of what he may have heard about you, but also because of what he may know about your firm through hearsay or past dealings?

Ask yourself, what are the most *negative* expectations he might develop about you before talking with you? Will he fear that you will be evasive? That you will try to "pin him to the wall"? That you want to "sell him something"? That you will want to do most of the talking?

TAKING COMMAND OF THE SITUATION

As you observe the other man during the opening moments of the confrontation, try to pick up clues to his preconceptions. Does he tend to tighten up whenever you get going? Does he seem to have an assumption that he can control the interview and that you will follow wherever he takes you? Get a line on his predisposition.

And then—break his preconception in a way that reflects creditably on you. If he seems to expect that you will be docile and passive, *take command*. . . "Before we get on to that sub-ject, I'd like to handle this other topic." If he anticipates that you will play it close to the vest about disclosing important facts, lay your cards on the table early. . . "I think we should talk on a basis of complete openness, so here are the facts and figures that will help me to be perfectly frank with you."

Here is an example of a manager putting this technique into action. Ken Graff has just taken over as sales manager. He is meeting for the first time since the change with Rudy Delman, head of the credit department. In the past, there has been a history of strife between sales and credit; Graff's predecessor was constantly at odds with Delman. The previous sales manager demanded that Delman be more liberal in accepting questionable orders. Delman insisted that the salesmen were always selling all kinds of bad risks, and then expecting them to be okayed.

Graff has a handful of orders that have been questioned or turned down by Delman. The credit man eyes the papers warily, and waits for Graff to launch into a tirade. But Graff says, "Before we go into these specific orders, Rudy, I'd like to get your thinking on the principles that salesmen should follow in sizing up an account in terms of credit. What advice would you pass along to them?"

Surprised, Delman clears his throat, and then talks about some of his ideas. Graff follows closely, making notes. Then the sales manager says, "Thanks, Rudy. This will be very helpful to me. Now, if you have time, let's go over these orders. Here's the first one, from Tad Wolper in Dallas . . . the Green Company."

Delman inhales, getting ready to deliver his negative opinion of that particular order and the salesman who wrote it. But Graff anticipates him: "On the basis of what we've been discussing, I agree with you. This order is not acceptable. But I want to give Wolman some guidelines for the future on deals like this. If I draft a letter to him, will you go over it?"

Delman says that he will. By now the credit manager has lost most of his suspicion of Graff. The meeting continues, with Delman approving a surprisingly high percentage of orders he had previously turned down.

A PLAN FOR MAKING A FAVORABLE IMPRESSION

The way in which you surprise the other party, or act counter to his negative preconceptions, will form the basis of the favorable impression he gets of you.

Here are the simple steps in assuring that you "come across" in interpersonal relationships in the way you want:

1. Anticipate the ways in which the other party is likely to have "typed" you. Form a rough idea of what he expects you to do and say.

2. Focus on the negative aspects of his preconception—the behavior that he is most apprehensive about, or that he is most apt to dislike.

3. Check on your estimate of his preconception during the first few seconds of conversation.

4. Early in the confrontation, take a definite step that contradicts his expectations in a way that will be reassuring or pleasant in his eyes.

There is no way to eliminate the human tendency to type people—in yourself or in others. But by recognizing the existence of the tendency, overcoming it in yourself and making it work *for* you in others, you can make the impression you want and need to make.

USING PSYCHOLOGICALLY SOPHISTICATED
QUESTIONS TO CONTROL THE INTERVIEW

Psychologists and psychiatrists achieve their functions by getting people to tell them things in a number of ways. We do not always say directly what is on our minds, particularly when the subject is sensitive, or when we fear that by disclosure we are giving the other party an advantage over us. So professionals must penetrate to the truth behind the words by observing not just what is said, but how it is said, and what is left out. Time is another factor that merits important consideration. If a psychologist had the luxury of unlimited time to spend with a subject, such as weeks and weeks, he would no doubt finally get everything he needed out of the other party. But that kind of time is not available. The professional must find out what he needs to know from someone who may not be eager to disclose it, and he must do it within a reasonably short time.

So psychologists, and others who need to learn about people by talking with them, must *control the interview*—steer it in the necessary direction and keep it on the right track. Moreover, this must be done subtly, because when the other person suspects he is being controlled, he will naturally resent the fact and balk.

Similar problems confront you in your face-to-face relationships with people in business. Your interview has a purpose; that purpose must usually be accomplished by drawing information out of the other party. You must do this effectively, which means it must be done without letting him know what is going on. And the process cannot take unlimited time. In business particularly, time is money, and contacts that run on too long are not only unproductive, but they are counter-productive. When a man classifies you as a time-waster, you are not in a very good position to pursue your relationship with him on a face-to-face basis.

So in your outside contacts, you want to. . .

   . . . control the interview;
   . . . get what you want out of the interview;
   . . . keep the time span of the interview to a minimum.

To some people, "controlling the interview" means seizing the conversational ball in a death grip, and trying hard never to relinquish it. But this is not controlling the interview; it is *strangling* the interview.

HOW THE PROFESSIONALS DO IT

Professional interviewers know that the interview is best controlled, with maximum productivity, by letting the other fellow talk, and gently guiding him so that he talks about the things you want to cover.

The way to do this is by adroit questioning.

The wrong kind of question can stop an interview in its tracks. Questions that require a premature yes-or-no answer; that seem to put the other person on the spot; that indicate the questioner is thinking primarily of himself . . . these are the types of queries that can push the conversation into a dead end.

So psychologists don't question in that fashion. They ask questions that. . .

. . . are open-ended—permitting the answer to flow on;
. . . avoid direct confrontation;
. . . and that indicate the questioner's interest in the other person by encouraging the other person to talk about himself.

The key to psychologically sound questioning that keeps the interview headed where you want it to go lies in two simple words —*you* and *we*. At first, the emphasis should be on *you*—so that the responder feels comfortable in saying "I" feel or think, or want such and such. As the interview progresses, there should usually be a shift over to emphasis on *we* in questioning, so that the questioner and responder answer the question jointly to their mutual benefit.

SIX QUESTIONS
THAT LET YOU CONTROL ANY INTERVIEW

Here, briefly, are six prototype questions that, adapted to the circumstances, can control an interview and keep it in the desired path:

1. What are your problems?
2. What would *you* like to see happen?
3. What do *you* see as actually happening?
4. How do *you* feel about the situation?
5. How can *we* work together to achieve the best possible result?
6. Where do *we* go from here?

Here's how these prototype questions might work to control an interview. Manager Axel Roth has been trying to get another manager, Mal Griffin, to work with him on a new setup that will expedite a freer flow of equipment and material from Griffin's storage bins to Roth's production area. Griffin has been dragging his feet. Now Roth begins to use the six-question method:

Roth: "I know it's tough for you to keep tabs on everything going in and out, Mal—and yet you're accountable. It must be a headache."

Griffin: "Sure is. If I didn't keep the lid on, these guys would strip me clean—and I wouldn't have a clue about where it's going."

Roth: "And yet, of course, you want to keep the line operations supplied with what they need. What would be an ideal setup, in your estimation?"

Griffin: "Something that would get the transactions handled as fast as possible with a minimum of paperwork and without having guys hanging around my bins all the time."

Roth: "I guess that's not the way it works now. . ."

Griffin: "Hell, no. Sometimes it looks like Grand Central Station. And when we ask a question about some scrawled requisition that nobody can read, the guys complain that we are holding up the works."

Roth: "What do you think it will take to straighten things out?"

Griffin: "The production guys have to take more responsibility to make out the requisition right. And they should realize that we can't fill ten orders at once."

Roth: "Well, what could we do on our end to help you?"

Griffin: "Some of your guys are all right. But a couple of them, Walters and Silva for instance, just want to breeze in and get the stuff themselves. You've got to get them out of the habit."

Roth: "Okay. And I wonder how you feel about this. If we set up a system where every requisition is checked, and where only one man at a time goes to your shop, that ought to cut down on the time and the confusion. . ."

Roth is controlling the interview and moving it along the desired path. He has used adaptations of the six basic questions.

THE ART OF LISTENING

Psychologically adroit questioning requires *listening* to the answers. Too many people overlook that; they are busy framing the next question. Listen—not only to what he says, but to what he does *not* say, or what he implies. When a man leaves out something that, under ordinary circumstances, would be included, there is a reason. He may be touchy about it; he may not have the answer, or feel that you will not like the answer. Here it is a good idea to ask the unanswered question of *yourself*. . . "One problem that occurs to me. . ." Then answer it and immediately ask, "How do you feel about that?"

Stick with the principle of sound questioning to be sure of interpersonal contacts that go where you want them to without engendering resentment or resistance from the other individual.

A STRONG PSYCHOLOGICAL TECHNIQUE
FOR WINNING AGREEMENT

In most business contacts, *persuasion* sooner or later becomes an important factor. You want to persuade the other person to undertake a particular course of action; or to stop doing something; or just to adopt a point of view that is more favorable to your interests.

Any manager who has been pursuing his profession for any length of time has developed certain standard techniques of persuasion. If he is a gifted persuader he will vary his approach to the circumstances and the personality and attitudes of the man he is trying to influence.

There is no cut-and-dried method of bringing another person around to your point of view. It is not our purpose to suggest any step-by-step method of persuasion.

But there *is* some new and highly interesting psychological research that bears upon a more fundamental and perhaps more important question. . . *What is the best way to create a psychological climate in which a man is most likely to be persuaded?*

But now there are some findings that lead us to a different and, we believe, important conclusion about the proper way to establish the "climate of consent."

The research was conducted by John P. Lombardo, Robert Frank Weiss, and William Buchanan at the University of Oklahoma. They set out to learn more about the circumstances under which one party can be brought to a point where he is attracted to a second party and, by extrapolation more willing to be persuaded by the other party. Pairs of individuals were brought together. In each pair, one of the parties was instructed as to how he should respond to certain points on which the other person was trying to persuade him.

In one group, the tactic was *agreement* right from the start. In a second group, the second party *disagreed* with the subject, and stuck to that disagreement. In yet a third group, the individuals to be persuaded disagreed at first, but then *yielded,* permitting themselves to be persuaded.

Results showed that the subjects had a significantly more positive response to those who agreed with them than to those who disagreed with them. But a markedly more positive response was noted in cases where the other individual *disagreed* at first, but then yielded after further persuasion.

Our own observations bear out the results of this research. In a business transaction, Smith will be more attracted to Jones, and subsequently more susceptible to persuasion by Jones, if Smith has been able to persuade Jones to come around to his own way of thinking on some point. This is not the case when Jones agrees with Smith right from the beginning.

Partially this seems due to what we might call a "fair exchange" psychology. Jones has demonstrated that he is willing to change his mind when presented with convincing evidence, so the onus is on Smith to show that he will do no less. In a measure, too, Jones' yielding to argument shows that Jones is, after all, a reasonable man, and therefore worthy of belief and trust. Then also, Smith's ego has been stroked by his ability to persuade Jones, and so Smith is in a somewhat more relaxed frame of mind then he would be otherwise.

These effects do not come into play if Jones agrees with Smith right from the start. When that is the case, Smith's victory is so easy that it may not occur to him that there has been any accommodation at all from the other side. Or, it may seem to him that Jones is just being a "yes man," currying favor in order to get agreement on his own point.

In order to create the "climate of consent" in your dealings with others, you can follow the principle indicated by these findings. People are more easily persuaded by and attracted to those who have at first disagreed with them, but then later have come round to a posture of agreement—rather than by those who stick to disagreement or those who agree right away.

You will quickly detect a point on which you disagree with the other party—but trying for agreement would damage your main concern in the interview. Your inclination may be to "throw away" this point—but don't do it. Let the other man marshal his arguments; hear them out; raise questions—and then agree to his point of view. Your agreement should not be abrupt; this leads to the suspicion based in the old axiom that

> "A man convinced against his will
> Is of the same opinion still."

Rather, your acquiescence should grow naturally out of your listening to and understanding the arguments that the other party is making. And this need not be a cynical or phony process; pay attention to what he is saying, look for the merit in it—and permit yourself to be persuaded.

When you have yielded to the other man's arguments, you have taken a significant stride toward establishing the "climate of consent" in which he is much more likely to give weight to your own point of view on a subject which is central to your purpose. And when you have created an atmosphere in which a man is willing to let himself be persuaded, you are well on the road to successful persuasion—whatever particular techniques you may apply.

HOW TO DEAL WITH OUTSIDERS

Here are the keynotes to fruitful dealings with customers and others outside your organization. . .

   . . . Size up the other person *as he is today* by watching and listening;

   . . . Come across with impact and effectiveness by "surprising" him with a more favorable action in a particular area than he anticipated;

   . . . Use psychologically sound questioning, emphasizing you and we, to guide and control the interview;

   . . . Establish the "climate of consent" by permitting yourself to be persuaded by him.

All of these steps are grounded in the new psychology; all are adaptable to the solution of important problems in interpersonal dealings.

10

New Techniques for Dealing with Problem People

We often hear managers say that they wished the only problems they had to face were planning, production scheduling, goal setting, and the like. Those problems are easier to deal with than the often messy difficulties presented by troublesome employees.

You have to be able to cope with *problem people*. Here are some recommendations for modern "people management," based on insights stemming from recent research.

THE WOMANIZER

Bill Kates was moving rapidly up the ladder at Midland Life. He was slated for top management, not only because of outstanding sales performance, but also because he was very personable. He was already a sales manager, and being groomed for an executive appointment to the home office. However, it was becoming increasingly apparent that sales success was only one of his accomplishments.

Bill apparently looked too good, at least for his career. His successes with women were gaining great notoriety, and Bill was quick to let many of his colleagues know of his conquests. His accomplishments with women were not a product of his fantasy, as everyone who travelled with him knew. Finally, his reputation managed to reach two important people, his boss and his wife.

Bill's marriage was headed toward the rocks, and his marital difficulties disrupted his work performance. His boss, Paul Miller, grew uncertain about promoting him. First, Paul heard of Bill's reputation from an executive of another company, and he was worried about potential embarrassment to the department and company. In addition, Miller was distressed by the change in Bill's work performance, and he was uncertain of the lasting affects of Bill's personal situation.

Paul was in a real dilemma. Should he talk to Kates about the problems? Or were they outside his responsibility? If he talked with him, how would he try to straighten out the problem without becoming too personal?

Here's how Miller handled it. He arranged to get together with Kates over lunch. Then, after some preliminaries, he began to talk frankly: "Bill, your private life is none of my business. But the way you handle yourself on the job *is* my business. When your work falls off, I have to look for reasons and see what I can do to help. In your case, Bill, I don't have to look very far for the trouble. I don't have to spell it out, do I?"

Kates was irritated, but he listened as Miller went on. "I've got two worries about you at the moment. One, your present performance. It has fallen off; you know as well as I do what you're capable of, and you know how far you're falling short. It's hurting the department. The second problem is the future—yours, mine, the department's, the company's. I have to be able to plan for some strong management talent if we're going to meet the goals we've set for the next five years. I want to be able to count on you. Until recently I thought I could; but now I have doubts. My job is to try to resolve these problems. Are you willing to work with me to help get them cleared up?"

Kates agreed that he was willing. Miller came to the crux of his argument: "The problem is you and women, Bill. At the moment the big hangup is the trouble your marriage has gotten into. I'm not a preacher and I'm not a psychologist. I know enough to know what I *don't* know. But there are people who do know about these things, and who have been able to help other guys who've gotten into fixes like yours. Would you be willing to consider getting some expert help?"

After some talk, Kates bought the idea that he and his wife, if she agreed, might benefit by consulting a marriage counselor. Miller had obtained the names of a few reputable professionals. Bill Kates went to one.

There were no overnight miracles, but gradually things began to work out. Now, Bill Kates and his wife are together again. Kates is performing up to his former standards. And both he and Paul Miller have moved into jobs with greater responsibility and higher salaries.

A PLAN FOR DEALING WITH THE WOMANIZER

Paul Miller followed a few simple guidelines in helping his problem subordinate to get straightened out.

1. *Stay out of employees' personal lives—except when they affect the job.* You will be called upon, more and more, to manage people with whose "life styles" you may disagree. If they do their jobs properly, and do not adversely affect others, their private lives are their own business. But when the work is involved, you have to accept responsibility.

2. *Talk frankly on a job-oriented basis.* When you talk with the woman-chaser, make it clear that your only concern is performance. Spell out the ways in which you see his predilections affecting his work or the work of others.

3. *Get agreement that it's a problem.* Until the employee concedes that there is work-involvement in his womanizing, nothing more can be done.

4. *Persuade him to seek professional help.* Some bosses try to psychoanalyze their workers. It's a mistake; the boss is not qualified to do it. Instead, get the employee to agree to obtain qualified counseling. Don't recommend any single professional; if you mention the names of any counselors at all, offer a choice of several.

THE PROBLEM DRINKER

Alcohol may be the single most destructive substance affecting our lives today. When a worker's drinking is affecting his work, the manager faces a problem. He wants to help, and his responsibility requires that he do something. But what?

Here are two brief cases of managers, each handling a subordinate's drinking problem in a different way.

Ted Johanssen liked his key assistant, Fred Untermeyer. Fred was a likeable guy. There was nobody more entertaining at a convivial lunch, or more the "life of the party" at office functions. Sure, Fred liked to drink, and occasionally he might have one more Scotch than prudence would dictate. But what was the harm in that?

Then it began to get a little more serious. Fred started taking two hours and more for "lunch," and came back in no shape to conduct business. Then he began to duck out in the morning for a "cup of coffee," returning, half an hour later, a little the worse for wear.

After observing this for a while, Ted took Untermeyer aside. "Fred, everybody likes a drink now and then. But we have to be careful. People around the office are starting to say, frankly, that your drinking is affecting your work." And so on; Ted talked to his assistant like a Dutch uncle, and Fred was contrite. He promised to watch it.

For a week or so it got better. But then Fred Untermeyer began to slip again. This time it was more serious . . . he was disappearing for entire afternoons, not coming to work at all for days at a time. Ted Johanssen spent a lot of time with Fred. He listened to the subordinate's troubles, even lent him some money. The big thing in Ted's mind was that this bright and talented worker must be saved. So he listened, counselled gently, and continued to hope. Unhappily, things did not seem to be getting better. They were getting worse. Fred Untermeyer promised to go to AA; perhaps he did, because for a couple of weeks he was sober. But, finally, after Fred had made a catastrophic drunken appearance at a meeting, Ted Johanssen sat at his desk and faced the fact that his subordinate and friend could not be reclaimed.

Over in another department, manager Phil Brinkley had a very similar problem. One of his section heads, a well-liked veteran named Cas Dill, was drinking too much to do himself or anyone else any good. After Dill failed to show up for a vital conference one afternoon, Brinkley called him in. The usually genial Brinkley was cool and remote. He warned Dill that the performance should not be repeated.

Dill kept on drinking. Brinkley confronted him again. This time he was downright tough. "This is the last warning, Cas. Either you stay sober on the job or you're through." Cas Dill began to talk about his problems with his wife, his worries about money, his feelings of loneliness and getting old, his worries about the future, etc. Brinkley waved it away. "I don't want to hear about it," he said. "This is the message. Get straightened out or I'm going to fire you."

And Cas Dill *did* get straightened out. Sure, he resented his boss' attitude. He went around telling people that Brinkley was pulling rank on an old friend. But Dill somehow managed to get his drinking under control. Maybe he still has a problem; but Phil Brinkley doesn't know about that. All he knows is that Cas Dill is, once again, a functioning member of his team.

A PLAN FOR STRAIGHTENING OUT
THE EMPLOYEE WHO DRINKS TOO MUCH

Organizations like the National Council on Alcoholism have concluded that many of the traditional attitudes toward the problem drinker that have been held by managers are wrong.

Managers with the laudable desire to be "human" often go easy on the problem drinker, particularly if he is an employee who has been around awhile. They try to counsel him in fatherly fashion. They listen to his tales of woe and agree that he has it tough. They overlook increasingly deplorable work because they don't want to load any more worries on the man who is going through such a tough period. We have known managers who will even go out and have a few drinks with an overly bibulous sub-ordinate. "I feel sorry for the guy," said one typical executive. "I look at him, understand the strains he is undergoing, and figure that there, but for the grace of God, go I."

But new explorations into the situation give us very strong indications that this is the exact wrong way to handle the drinker. Problem drinkers develop great ingenuity in coming up with ex-cuses for themselves; this is part of the psychology of the alco-holic. And one of the most prevalent rationales used by the problem drinker—to his wife, to his friends, to himself—is the assertion that he is "still able to hold a job." Holding on to the job becomes, therefore, all-important. It is the drinker's assurance that he is really not in such bad shape after all; that the problem is not enormous; that he "has it under control." Since he con-tinues to hold his job, he rationalizes that he is still a functioning individual who has lost none of his basic manhood.

When a solicitous boss bends over backwards to keep on reas-suring such a person, the drinker is supported in his unwillingness to realize the truth and his continuation of a destructive habit. Since his manager gives no indication of being sore at him, or implies no threat of firing, the problem drinker can retain the comfortable pattern of drinking too much and then promising to reform. The situation keeps on going downhill until the employee is practically a basket case, and drastic action becomes unavoid-able.

But, if the boss gets tough, then he has a chance of reaching the subordinate who is suffering from this widespread malady. When the boss states clearly that a continuation of present be-havior will soon lead to termination, the drinker's ability to rationalize his own behavior will often be severely shaken. It may take some really blunt talk by the manager to get through to him; problem drinkers are even more prone than most of us to hear only what they want to hear, particularly after they have had a few drinks. Nevertheless, the manager should go out of his way to deliver the message, loud and clear: "If you don't shape up soon you are through."

So, paradoxically, to be kindest to a problem drinker, and to perform the task of management most effectively, it is necessary for you to crack down hard.

STEPS FOR HANDLING THE SUBORDINATE
WITH A DRINKING PROBLEM

1. *Keep an eye on the employee who "likes a few drinks."* He may be able to handle it; he may not. Don't assume that, because he has been able to do his job while drinking, that he can continue to do so. Watch him.

2. *Maintain standards of performance.* When drinking makes an employee unduly late or causes a slowdown in his work, call him to account. Avoid the temptation to give him a break; by taking it easy on him, you may be doing the opposite.

3. *Talk to him only when he is sober.* When he's been drinking, he may welcome the opportunity for a maudlin conversation. Brush him off. But get him the next morning, when he may not be altogether up to par, but when he will be sober.

4. *Keep your talk work-oriented.* Concentrate on his performance. Cite specific instances in which he is not measuring up.

5. *Point out the consequences of continuation of the pattern.* Get the message across: "If this goes on, I will be forced to terminate you." If and when he offers excuses or talks about his problems, say, "I'm sympathetic, but we all have a job to do here."

6. *Set a time limit.* Give the employee a deadline—one not too far in the offing.

7. *Be specific about your demands.* Spell out what you expect in terms of application to the job, attitude, and output.

8. *Require that he seek help.* Don't become his psychoanalyst. Tell him to go to someone who can offer him professional assistance. Be ready with suggestions if he wants them. *But*—make it plain that just his promise to seek help, or his actual seeking of that help, is *not* enough. (Some drinkers will consult a psychologist—and then just keep on drinking.) Reiterate that the only thing that will save his job is a return to acceptable performance.

GETTING THE OVERLY "NICE" GUY TO DO HIS JOB

Fulton Chemical has a policy of promotion from within. Tom Seely was promoted from a production job in the home chemical division to a foreman position in industrial chemicals.

Tom was doing very nicely as a foreman in the new division for about six to eight months, but around that time his boss, Leon Klein, started to notice that production was falling off. The work group seemed to be unruly and undisciplined.

Klein questioned Seely directly about what was happening, and with particular reference to the drop off in production. Tom could offer no explanation. He tried to convince his boss that it was temporary, and noted that he was particularly pleased with the rapport he had established with his subordinates. Klein was not satisfied, and he spoke with three or four of the workers whom he had known. The consistent response was that "Tom is a great guy; not like a boss."

Now Leon Klein had a real problem. On the one hand, he was reluctant to destroy Tom Seely's rapport with his people. But Tom was getting too close to his subordinates; "rapport" had slopped over to the extent that Seely's leadership role was being seriously compromised.

Klein decided to try a remote approach. After careful thought, he composed a long memo to Tom Seely, spelling out the requirements of the supervisory job and his approved philosophy of supervision. Tom thanked him, and said he had read it with great interest. But there was no improvement.

Then Klein tried a somewhat more direct approach. Spotting Tom in the hall, he asked him to drop in for a chat. Klein went on for some time about the fine spirit he had observed in Tom's group. Then Klein posed a somewhat hesitant question—"But, Tom, do you really feel that you're able to maintain a position of authority with all of your gang? I mean, it's great to be a boss that they like, but what about the times when you have to say things that are unpopular?" Seely said confidently that everything was okay; and that was the end of that.

After getting some more negative reports from Seely's area,

Klein decided that a more direct approach was necessary. He notified Tom in advance, setting the time and establishing the agenda. When Tom arrived, looking a bit concerned, Klein dispensed with the pleasantries quickly, and got right down to cases: "Tom, here are last month's figures. They're not good. I'd like to hear your comments."

Seely offered various excuses, but Klein was unwilling to be put off. He pursued the point that some of Tom's people were just not producing as well as they should, and he asked Tom what he was doing about it. Tom replied somewhat lamely that he was "talking to them."

"Have you told them to 'shape up or ship out' "? Klein asked. Tom said that he did not favor this tough approach. And now Klein went on to say, "Tom, in being easy on your people you are destroying your own reputation." He spelled out the performance he wanted out of the department, and suggested that Tom must toughen up in order to attain it. Finally, Klein said, "I realize you've worked hard to establish good relationships, and I'm not suggesting that you turn into 'Mr. Hyde' overnight. But I do suggest you become a lot more firm in demanding performance. I will back you up, and do what I can to take undue heat off you. But you will have to get used to taking heat yourself. It comes with the title." It was not long after this interview that the production curve in Seely's area began to move up again.

SOME SIMPLE RULES FOR STRAIGHTENING OUT THE SUBORDINATE WHO IS TOO EASY-GOING

The indirect "soft" approach that Leon Klein took to this problem is one that held popular sway among managers a few years ago. But the experience of the 1970's has taught us some new lessons. Here is a suggested method of dealing with this kind of employee.

1. *Don't handle the matter indirectly through memos, telephone calls or an interested third party.*

A face-to-face interview is called for. Every experienced manager knows about the importance of privacy; the importance of the right time of day, neither too early nor too late; and the importance of a sufficient period for a relaxed discussion, and absolute freedom from interruption.

2. *Prepare for the interview carefully—and be businesslike.*
The interview is taking place because performance has been hurt. The facts should be put together beforehand. The case should be approached objectively without, at first, bringing up the personal problem. The manager might say, in effect:

"Bill, your work has fallen off." Or, you don't seem to be able to get the needed cooperation from people." Specific evidence should be cited, and the more measurable the better: Number of sales, percent decrease in production, specific cases of alienation.

Then the man should be asked if he can suggest why. If possible, let him bring up his personal problem. In a surprising number of cases he will. And frequently he will be relieved to talk to someone about it.

If he does not introduce the subject, the manager must. But he must not moralize about it. The manager's only goal is to restore the man's effectiveness, and his personal problems should be discussed only as a barrier to his effectiveness.

3. *Avoid the "sandwich" technique. This means, of course, a slice of critical comment between two slabs of praise.*
The boss calls in the subordinate, hands him a cigar, then tells him what a great job he's doing. Then shifting gears, he edges into the subject. Then he shifts back into amiability and the subordinate is sent on his way.

Squeamish bosses feel that the "sandwich" approach is a way to handle the situation tactfully. It isn't. At best, it leaves the subordinate confused.

4. *Follow up by doing what you can—within reason—to assist the problem worker's efforts to cope with his difficulty.*

A GENERAL APPROACH TO PROBLEM PEOPLE

Problem employees come in all shapes and sizes. At any given moment, you may find your professional life plagued by the office politician; the jungle-fighter; the back-stabber; the crisis-creator; and a host of other disruptive personalities.

When confronted with such problem people, managers typically fall into particular categories. At one extreme is the do-it-yourself psychoanalysis man who is never so happy as when he is playing God, advising people about any and all personal hang-ups. At the other extreme is the manager who proclaims that he never gets involved in a personal problem—"I wouldn't touch it with a ten foot pole!"

Your ideal approach lies between these two extremes.

The question, then, is when to step in, or when should the manager get into the act?

The subordinate's problems must be considered in the context of his job, and what the job means to the organization. No matter how distasteful or distressing the individual's behavior may be, this alone is never sufficient reason to intervene. Indeed, to take action on such grounds is asking for trouble.

This is what the yardstick should be: Are the employee's personal problems causing discernible negative effect upon his work or that of others? Is his behavior embarrassing the company in any way? If the answer is "Yes," then the manager has the right and responsibility to act.

There are telltale behavior signs that stem from personal problems. Four of the most common are:

Hostility—The man lashes out at others for no apparent reason. People "can't get along with him." Meetings and conversations that should be routine become highly charged because of the individual's excessive touchiness.

Indecisiveness—He cannot make up his mind. He is never certain about anything. His mind is elsewhere; he has not absorbed the background facts. Or, his confidence is impaired; he is afraid to take a risk.

Inappropriate response—He does the wrong thing. He gets

drunk at meetings. He is lackadaisical at moments of crisis. He cannot seem to judge things in their proper proportions. He is unable to differentiate the important from the unimportant challenges, and thus ignores a critical challenge while overworking a petty detail.

Destructiveness—He is destroying himself through promiscuity or alcohol. He tries to destroy others through indulgence in cutthroat politics. He tears down the organization and the people who work with him by irresonsible talk and, sometimes, action.

However, when the problem is identified, certain precautions and limitations must be pointed out. The person's neurosis will not yield to pep talks. Psychotherapists know that the processes involved in resolving many personal problems are much more complex than a pep talk.

This then leads to the next precaution. The manager should recognize that he is not a therapist. If a person seems in need of professional help, the manager may recommend it, but he should not attempt to provide it.

Discretion is of great importance, if only because there are many legal angles. Managers who deal carelessly in personal problems may leave themselves or the company open to a lawsuit. It is a good idea to check things out with a legal adviser.

Modern management is a demanding occupation. Things happen fast. People work under stress. The stakes on management decisions are critically high. The people the manager must deal with often seem fractious and uncooperative. Every aspect of supervising people has come to appear highly complex.

All too often, the contributions of behavioral scientists have tended to complicate these complexities rather than clarify them. The manager knows that there are new developments in the leadership and understanding of people, but he can't understand the jargonized versions of these developments as they are presented to him. So it is not surprising that he comes to mistrust his own instincts, relying on money as his principal motivator and adopting a "hands-off" attitude, instead of trying to get people to perform better. This situation is the opposite of what psychological research should accomplish. In this book, we have reviewed the important discoveries that are emerging today and put them in a context designed to give the manager specific tools for solution of his problems.

One of the vital threads running through the book is the concept that employees can be made more effective *without* resort to copious transfusions of payroll dollars. Many people want to be told what to do—if the manager does the telling in the right way. Many people are willing to work harder—if they are reached by the right appeal. Workers will respond to strong leadership—if they understand how this response fosters their own self-interest.

Another important point—the manager can and should trust his basic instincts more readily. It is not "unscientific" to play a hunch at times; in fact, rigorous investigation now shows us that this can be the one best course of action under a variety of circumstances.

Employees are not easy to figure out. Today we realize that we can never fully know any human being, including ourselves. But this does not mean that the manager cannot develop his perceptions to the point at which he knows enough about his people to make decisions with confidence and accuracy. This book has presented some newly-developed methods that can be used by anyone in a supervisory position. They will not provide full knowledge, but will provide enough insight to run a business operation with more work and less waste.

The speed and stress of modern business calls for positive management action that is flexible enough to respond fast to changing situations. The manager who takes advantage of the tools that are becoming available to him is the manager who will stand out today—and in the days to come.

Index

193